Gypsy NoMad Hippie Chick
Homeless In New Hampshire

Dana Vilandre

Copyright © 2020
All Rights Reserved

ISBN: 978-1-7345704-1-0

Dedication

Gypsy NoMad Hippie Chick was written for the ladies of Her Place. I will always be grateful for your support and kindness when my tears were too heavy for tissues to hold.

Much love,

Dana

Contents

Dedication i
~Gypsy NoMad Hippie Chick~ 1

Chapter One - A Day in the Life of a Fisherwoman 2
~Let Me Hold Your Hand~ 24

Chapter Two - A Gypsie NoMad Hippie Chick 25
    August 18, 2010 25
    Sept 18th, 2010 27
~The Journey~ 30

Chapter Three - Time to Write 32
~Some Mornings Just Happen~ 45

Chapter Four - Such an Ordinary Life 47
~Somedays~ 49

Chapter Five - Defining Mr. Right 50
~Assholeness~ 58

Chapter Six - One Summer Day 60
Words... Are Just Experience with A Meaning Defining Them . 69

Chapter Seven - Friendships 70
A Piece of Glass 81

Chapter Eight - Let Live. Let's Love 83
~Transference~ 90

Chapter Nine - Resolve 92
~I Had A Complaint~ 100

Chapter Ten - David's Corner *102*
~Sorry... I'm Conboozed~ *112*

Chapter Eleven - The Band *114*
~A Date~ *121*

Chapter Twelve - The Book of James *122*
~Butterfly~ *128*

Chapter Thirteen - Roula's Restaurant *129*
~The Dino~ *135*

Chapter Fourteen - Dancing with Mary *137*
~How to make a snowman~ *147*

Chapter Fifteen - No Price Tags, No Paychecks *149*

~Gypsy NoMad Hippie Chick~

Been a bit of a Gypsy for awhile
Feeling it is time to come back home
Then something else seems to come down my path
And again I find myself being told to roam.
Beautiful nights, dream-filled days
Make the unpaved road I am on the only path I want to see
Might as well enjoy the new phase
Healing from a broken heart, financial pains, and life-shifting cycles
Teaching me every day who I am meant to be.
Finding I have been given a brand-new start
To be the woman, the shapeshifter, dyno mom, mad ass cool
With lots of charm.
Having fun making friends
Helping weed the garden
Mend the fence. Healing from the harm...
Now this Gypsy NoMad Hippie Chick is setting free
The judgments of this silly-ass world...
It is time to just be...
~Me~

Chapter One
~A Day in the Life of a Fisherwoman~

She felt the panic rising up in her chest. *Was she making the right decision?* She thought again to herself. What else was she supposed to do? She started working her way through her 'version' of the Our Father again, trying to keep panic at bay.

Our Father, Guider, Storyteller, she thought to herself.

Her mind kept drifting back to the night ahead. *Thought control*, she thought to herself for the millionth time. *Worrying won't change a thing.*

"Hey, are you okay?"

She looked away from her view of the boat floor and up at Stephan. Stephan was looking at her concerned. Maybe he thought the waves were making her seasick.

"I'm okay. Just saying a prayer, you know..." Stephan was big on prayer, so she knew she could be candid with him. "Let's catch some mackerel and get back."

Once again, she thought of her decision to go out for more bait and continue fishing instead of heading back for class.

What was my other choice? she thought to herself.

She knew in her heart they weren't going to catch any stripers today. She could feel it in the pit of her stomach. She took a deep breath, refocusing on her prayer.

How Holy is your name... You are amazing, God. She took a deep breath – the ocean air and the view before her attesting to her words.

This had become something of a game for her. This became her way of spending time with God, this 're-write' with which she had started to communicate her thoughts and ask for direction when she was living with some friends who had opened their home to her and her children. She had such a hard time calming down that she would go for long walks and think of what that prayer meant to her.

The fact her gas light was on, and she had a dollar in her wallet popped into her head again. Another wave of anxiety rose up in her chest.

The boat slowed to a roll as they reached the area they had earmarked for fishing mackerel.

She thought of her recent conversation with her friend about the last disappointing trip. It was hard to remember that her fear was not a new emotion. It seemed to be a constant companion this last year, though it seemed this situation didn't have a lot of alternatives.

She took another deep breath. In through the nose, out through the mouth.

She thought again of her decision to work for Stephan this summer for some money so she could continue with her studies. If things kept on like they were going so far, it would become their third outing with no fish coming back home. The conversation with the owner of the boatyard no longer gave her any comfort.

I swear I am reenacting every character in the Bible. She softly laughed to herself at the thought. Poor Stephan. He had made a comment that they needed a good catch today when they had finally started heading out after the trailer hitch fiasco this morning.

Throw me off the boat, she thought to herself, *you'll probably catch something then.*

No sense letting my issues sit on Stephan's shoulders, she thought, and got up, and smiled at Stephan.

"Alrighty then, let's catch us some bait!"

She really enjoyed fishing. It was so nice to sit in the sun with so much quiet. She loved the sounds around her and the calmness that she usually enjoyed.

There was a family fishing in a boat where they had stopped. Her mind drifted back to her friend. *He would love this.* Her breath caught a bit. *Dammit, what's worse? To think of him all day over everything or the fact I keep ending up in these financially stressful situations I try not to worry over?* She thought to herself. *Okay, deep breaths. Focus on the moment. There are no problems to be worried over if you are living toward being in the solution.*

She thought again about her gas light and having to drive tomorrow to get the kids for the weekend. Another wave of anxiety rose up in her chest.

Deep breaths, relax, fish.

They cast out, and she started catching some mackerel right away. Stephan and Christian weren't having much luck, but she wasn't focused on them.

Our Father, Provider, Protector, she started again. *Maybe if I can get through the whole thing without thinking of him or my instability, my heart will calm down,* she thought. *Damn, I wish I had some Scooby snacks.*

She had thought she could breathe for a bit this last semester, though once again, things took a different turn than she expected.

What am I going to do? She felt the wave of panic rise up hard in her chest again. *It is God's way of taking care of me; He always does. It's okay, what's the worst that can happen? I sleep in the boatyard, again?* She took a deep breath. That slightly relaxed her. She thought through this for a moment. Maybe Dick would have a boat to clean and he will front her money for gas. *Yes,* she thought. *That would be a reasonable request.*

I feel like such a loser, she thought to herself. She didn't want Stephan to know of her situation. He had already advanced her money for her car payment. Plus, since he asked her out and she turned him down as nicely as she could, even being on the boat felt awkward now.

They had drifted right next to the family that was fishing. She was startled at how close they suddenly were.

She had been lost among her thoughts.

Shit, the wife is blonde! She laughed a bit at herself and her new 'mantra' – that she did not hate blonde, well-off married women. She smiled and said a quick prayer for him and his family, trying to ignore the lump she felt in her throat.

"Okay, I think we should go with what we got and head out again," Stephan said, interrupting her battle of acceptance.

"I want to go out a couple of miles," he continued. She didn't think much of what he said. She didn't have a good concept of distance, so she hadn't realized they had always been fairly close to the shore.

Again, the boat took off. The ocean was getting choppy, and the boat would come off the waves extremely hard.

A hook came undone on one of the rods, and it flew close to Stephan's face.

"Should I go re-hook that?" she asked, thinking, *please say no,* as she looked at the water flying up onto the bow and how fast they were going. Christian was lying down in the cabin. He had been puking all day and would lie down when they rode. They were going so fast that her heart raced just thinking about it.

Water splashed over the windshield onto her face. "Yes," he said.

She hesitated a minute, hoping he would slow down. When she realized he wasn't planning to, she grabbed the edge of the windshield and stepped up onto the bow.

"Damn, my clumsy ass is nuts," she mumbled to herself as she worked her way to the front edge of the boat. Hanging on to the windshield with one hand, she reached out to let some line loose to re-hook it before tightening it. Her heart was racing. *My own fault,* she thought, *If I had thought through it, I would have known to tighten it so it wouldn't fall off.*

The boat slowed as she was finally stepping back into the captain's area.

"Holy Cripers, we are out far," she said out loud as they came to a stop. A wave came over the low edge of the back of the boat. She felt that familiar rise of fear in her chest.

"Okay, to let down?" She asked Stephan, refocusing on the task at hand. Dick had said it was unusual not to catch something for a commercial trip. The fish had been biting earlier. Only, none of the fish met size and they had to throw them back in.

The thought crossed her mind that she probably was not going to make it to her 8:10 class either. Just as well, since she was sure she smelled like fish. She hadn't thought through the shower situation. There were so many things for her to think of. This was a new situation for her. She honestly would not really have cared, although her thoughts went to Tony.

He had made it more than obvious he had an interest. He was incredibly hot, very buff, and tan. However, she just didn't have any desire to get involved with a player. She set that tone pretty quick by not using the number he gave her two days after their first meeting. Nevertheless, she had to admit, sharing the story he wrote about when his grandparents met in Italy was an impressive approach.

Anyway, she thought, *we won't get back in time regardless.* She felt a wave of anxiety as she thought of the assignment that was due tonight.

Another ocean wave came over the back of the boat. She felt her stomach lurch a bit. *Great, now I am going to have to worry about the boat tipping and sharks.* Her mind went back to the conversation with her friend. He always made her laugh. *Dammit,* she thought, *why do I keep doing this to myself? It's like a few minutes of pleasurable exchanges, and I read and re-read those words ten times over.*

Refocus, deep breaths, fish.

"Okay, pull up. We are going to head back and try the river again," Stephan yelled out. They hadn't had one bite.

She made sure her line was hooked tight and went and sat down. She felt shaky. The only offer for a place to stay this weekend with her children was in Holbrooke. Well, of those she would entertain. Her kids had made so many sacrifices this last year that she really tried to make every time with them the best she possibly could.

She knew it was a big change for them to adjust to her not having the money for the things they wanted or the typical, fun things they would normally do during summer vacation. She felt a bit of sorrow creep into her chest. *Deep breath. Just stop!* She thought. *It will work out. It always does.*

This was one of those moments of faith. *Shit, I can't even get through the flippen Lord's Prayer!* She thought to herself. She laughed a bit at how she just said shit and prayer together and the conversation she had had with the Sunday school teacher when she said missionary and fuck a couple of weekends ago. Well, how was she supposed to know she was a Sunday school teacher?

Stephan interrupted her train of thought. "Hey, do you see those boats over there? Those are extremely dangerous. They get tipped by waves all the time." She shuddered at the thought. Then she thought she should tell her friend about this. *Now, why should I tell him that?* She thought to herself. She thought again how frustrating it was to always think of him.

Refocus, breathe, fish.

"Okay, let's just drift here. Let down."

Right away, Christian had a fish on.

"Wow! This guy is big!" Christian yelled.

"Line in," Stephan yelled.

She reeled her reel in as fast as she could. Lately, she had no perception of time and she felt it took forever to do so. With the line finally in, she turned just as Christian let out a swear. His line had pulled up with half a fish on it.

She turned and let down; the disappointment felt throughout her chest. It really was the difference of one good size fish, Dick had said. She wished she was better with estimating numbers so she could understand what a good size fish would equate to in terms of a paycheck.

She looked at Stephan. He had been such a good friend to her. She wished she could communicate with him better. She had never met a man that was so difficult to communicate with, which made her really value the times she was able to spend with his teenage daughters. She smiled to herself, recalling a conversation she had with his oldest. Stephan was a great dad; he was just a horrible communicator.

When she first became friends with Stephan, he had been married. They were strictly friends, and he had never alluded to anything more. After he had gotten divorced, she had hoped she emphasized clearly that she was not interested in him as anything more than a friend. It was hard to do that because he never had actually said anything contrary to just that.

This made her think of Tuesday night and her frustrating thread of texts with him.

Well, he still let me come out with him today, she thought. *Though I wonder if he is superstitious.* She thought again about Jonah and the whale.

Shoot, where did I leave off? I wish I had something to help me relax. My brain is retarded, she thought to herself.

Thy kingdom come… She thought of the women's organization she had been creating. The latest line of conversations had a definite spiritual undertone – what a strange set of emotions this sparked within her when she thought of this.

I wish I knew more of how the women feel. The women never said much to her directly. She had been told they emailed each other, though she wasn't sure how much.

She thought of her friend and felt that familiar ache. She prayed for him and his family. She hated it when she thought of his marriage. She thought of his boys – the boys that are the boys that will be the future husbands to girls like her daughter. She prayed for her friend.

She thought of the company she was so impressed with and the college program they had in place. She prayed for the owner and his beautiful wife, for their company, and for

Bill. She smiled, thinking of Bill's response to the attorney's email, and wondered what their connection was going to form into.

"Okay, let's call it a day." She felt it to her core. *Okay, deep breaths, God has another plan.*

Please, God, don't let that plan involve Mike. She said a quick prayer because he was confusing to her. There were too many cracked prisms for her taste. She didn't like that she couldn't communicate with him on things that were hurtful to her without him verbally attacking her character. She knew when she walked out of his place on Wednesday, she wasn't going to go back.

She thought of her gas light being on, and another wave of anxiety came over her.

She needed to be sure she sent 'Sanctuary' in by email to her professor tonight since she missed class. She thought through this line of thought for a minute. She decided she will ask Dick if she can use his computer when she got back to the boatyard. She knew she had a copy of it already in her email.

Okay, breathe, relax.

The disappointment hung heavy in the boat.

Just as the boat pulled into the docking area, her phone went off. It was her son. She took a deep breath before opening it. *Stay calm,* she thought.

"What is the plan for this weekend?"

"Hey! Do you mind helping him?" Stephan yelled up to her. She felt a wave of guilt that she was texting instead of helping. She apologized and put the phone down. She jumped onto the dock and grabbed the rope to help steer her in.

She and Christian worked on docking the boat while Stephan went to get the boat's trailer.

"I feel sad we didn't catch anything," she said to Christian, regretting it immediately when it came out of her mouth.

He looked at her odd and said, "These trips are just fun for me. I don't think of them in terms of getting paid."

She agreed with him that it's the best job to get skunked from. She took a deep breath and said she was just upset because she wasn't sure what she would do now.

She let that trail off, realizing he was just a young kid and couldn't possibly understand what her situation meant. She excused herself and jumped back on the boat to retrieve her phone.

"We are planning to go to Holbrooke," she texted her son back. A wave of anxiety was pushing at her chest.

Now, where did I leave off with my prayer? She thought. *Okay, daily bread. Yes, no kidding, God.* She wondered if everyone experienced things as literal as this.

"We didn't catch any fish, so I am not sure." She paused a minute. Should she this send to him? She thought if she was not able to drive there to pick them up, he would handle it better if she gave him more information upfront.

She hit send just as Stephan showed up and started to back his trailer under the boat.

She grabbed her book bag, tossed her phone into it, and jumped back off the boat onto the dock.

She took a deep breath. *Calm down,* she thought to herself. *Things will work out.*

"Can you get in and drive the truck?" Stephan asked her.

"Sure," she smiled and ran around and jumped in.

"Just put it in third and go slow. We will yell when to stop," he yelled out to her.

"Okay," she replied. She remembered this from last time, though she didn't say so. Who cared?

They got the boat out, and she jumped out of the truck just as Christian and Stephan walked around the boat toward her. Christian was leaning in, talking to Stephan in a way that immediately gave away that they were talking about her. *Damn car guys, always telling a story,* she thought to herself as she ran around the truck and jumped in the back. They both worked full time for a dealership out in town.

She had too much going on to worry about what these two guys thought of her.

On the ride back, she tried to keep the truck upbeat. She told a couple of funny stories and gave a brief apology if she came off bitchy to feel better about her complaining. No sense bringing them down for her poor choices.

She thought again about where she left off in her prayer.

Forgive us our trespasses. Her thoughts immediately

went to her friend and his family. How hard it was to know that no matter how hard she tried to control her thoughts; they always went back to him. She wanted his home life to be a happy one, and she wanted him to be happy. She wondered if she would always feel this stab of jealousy when she thought of his wife. She said a prayer for his wife. She said a prayer for him. She prayed for them.

But now, she felt frustrated she couldn't seem to get through a prayer without something leading her mind back to him.

As we forgive those that... She refocused on the prayer. She was so different today. She wouldn't even know if he would like her if they were to hang out again. *Well, why even go down that line of thought?* She felt that lump in her chest again, and she took another deep breath.

"Hey, if you need to take off, I understand," Stephan turned from the driver's seat and looked at her. She knew the boat needed a hard scrub down. There was a lot of blood and chum all over it.

"No, I'm good. I just need to run in quickly and send an email to my professor and then I will come clean with you.

Can you drop me off in front please… so I can run in?"

"I will do better," Stephan said, "I will give you door-to-door service."

She smiled at him and said thank you.

She jumped out as Dick was getting out of his truck. "Hey Dick, can I use your computer for a minute to email my school?"

Did she sense a look of annoyance flash across his face? After all, she had used it this morning and had a cup of his coffee. "Go ahead, Mikey is in there," Dick said.

She smiled at him. "Thank you," she said.

"Catch anything?" He asked.

She felt the lump in her throat as she calmed herself down enough to answer. "No." She quickly walked away, suddenly feeling uncomfortable to ask about any cleaning work.

She went back into the office and opened the browser. Something was wrong. The browser wouldn't log onto Yahoo. *Oh, flip, how frustrating,* she thought as she put her head into her hands on the desk. *Deep breaths.*

She breathed. In through her nose, out through her mouth. *Calm down,* she thought. It's okay. Her teachers were fairly reasonable, and even though they didn't know the full extent of her situation, they knew she had some unusual circumstances. She felt better when she thought of how she could go to the library and explain it to them via email tomorrow.

Feeling a bit better, she got up and headed out into the yard.

She ran over to them just as they were unloading the last of the coolers onto the grass. She grabbed the hose and started filling soap-buckets.

She felt a bit dizzy and lightheaded. Her thoughts flashed to dinner, and she felt another wave of anxiety hit her. She grabbed a brush and started to wash down the coolers.

They worked hard and fast, scrubbing down the deck of the boat with bleach and a hard brush. She was covered in sweat by the time they were done.

She looked at Stephan. "I am going to take off," she said.

"Where are you going?" He asked her. Dick had walked over to talk to Christian, and the captain that runs Stephan's other boat had come over as well. Everyone looked at her.

"I am not sure yet," she said, swallowing down the lump of panic in her throat.

She left quickly, not wanting to break down in front of them all.

"Hey, I will be here for a couple more hours," Stephan yelled after her.

Yeah, I may be too, she thought, *overnight sleeping in Chrysler Concorde.* In spite of herself, she smiled. Her car was always a source of amusement for her.

Her phone, *Shit.* She had forgotten to charge it and it was draining. What else could possibly go wrong today? She took a deep breath, trying to calm her mind. *It will be okay. These are all not very big deals at all,* she thought to herself. *Challenging, yes, but life-threatening, no.*

She sat in the driver's seat, her head back, and eyes closed. *Refocus,* she thought, *refocus on the prayer.*

Lead us not into temptation. She sat and thought of her options. What were the choices she really had without compromising her integrity?

Deep breaths, calm down. Relax.

Should she call her friend? She thought back to just the Friday before. Less than a week ago, and she had had the same thought run through her mind. She thought of how she had sat and cried on the beach that last Friday morning, unsure of what to do. She hadn't had the full amount of the fine, which was due that following Monday, and she knew they wouldn't continue her case again. She hadn't been sure if she would have to spend a few days in jail to pay it off.

She thought through her decision to drive the hour-long distance and plead with the prosecutor. It had worked out in her favor that they had dropped the charge to a violation, and he had further reduced the fine to $150. She had $200 at the ready, so that had worked and had still given her gas to get back. She sat here now and knew in her heart she wouldn't ask her friend. She knew she would find another alternative rather than put either of them in an awkward position.

She started to cry. How many times has she felt this incredible sadness this last year? This constant back and forth dialog always going on in her brain. *And deliver us from evil...* She thought how many of her worst fears had been realized this last year, her own hell being her own thoughts themselves.

For thine is the kingdom, the power, and the glory forever. Amen.

Her phone went off. She looked down, and it was an old friend of hers, one who had decided to leave a relationship with a woman he had felt he loved, to get back with his wife and kids two years ago, after having been separated for four years. His reason for this being he was not able to see his kids all of the time. She felt a stab at the irony. He had been a very good friend, and though at one time they had considered dating, after he met Sonya, their friendship really solidified.

His wife didn't care for her, so when they got back together, her friendship with him had become strained. He wasn't happy with his decision, and he also battled with depression. She had not felt she could fill him in on her year without feeling like she was burdening him, so he hadn't really known what this year had been like for her. She took a deep breath. She felt very humbled as she typed the keys on her phone.

"I need help..."

~Let Me Hold Your Hand~

Let me hold your hand as you find your path to walk down, though my light went out, and I was blind in the darkness. Your anguish flashed across your face at my words, which I missed.
They flashed as though behind the scenes. Your true feelings were on your face in an instant. Not hidden, now were seen.
Let me walk beside you and we will hold our heads up high, and to you, my friend under my breath, I will continue to sing a lullaby.
I know others reached out when they heard my cry, the dark, the dark, by eyes so blind. Again, I could only see myself, my death defied, and I scrambled like a survivor on a buoy. A deep breath. I survived.
Humbled today, a whole new meaning of success now created in my mind. No longer drowning or captivated by the world's fancy jewels bellowing for my time.
As I live my world beside you, strangers yet sisters far and wide, and we search our own hearts and our own choices, our walks alone are ours to decide.
Let me hold your hand, in my heart, my soul there in spirit rather than in form. This metaphysical connection of understanding and strength, not to be pitied, not to feel torn.
A breath blown by angels as we will all get through, and figure out this crazy world, and then just enjoy the view…

Chapter Two
~A Gypsie NoMad Hippie Chick~

August 18, 2010

She sat by the fire, lost in thought. So many emotions were rushing through her mind at once. Pain, hurt, confusion, anger. Hate? She felt sad, lost to her situation. *How old am I?* She thought. *Is there any truth in others' criticism of me?* She felt lost, feeling herself struggle with what seemed to be the outcome of merely following her heart.

Could doing what I felt was the right thing be the truth in the words and judgment others have about me?

It was drizzling out. She sat alone in the drizzle with just her thoughts. She had no car to run away in. Her cell phone had no charge, so she couldn't find escape in other's problems – listening to their problems instead to divert her from her own. She had no desire to call anyone, regardless. She had not one ounce of willingness to hear someone say what she should have done differently.

She sat by the fire, keeping it burning all day and night. She sat and stared, lost in thought, lost in her feelings.

Is this it? Is this how it ends? She could feel the tears, the warmth of them on her cheeks was almost like a burning sensation against the cold from the drizzle. The things that have come to be in the last month certainly weren't the worst she had experienced throughout her life. She was not as alone as she had been in the past. But somehow, this time, it felt different. She felt drained and done. She felt judged without any real direction to help her situation sincerely. She willingly walked away from what she claimed she loved. Others felt she made her bed; she should lay in it.

Normally, she felt blessed with short-term memory, able to move on quickly from downfalls. She moved to the next situation without spending a lot of time thinking of the last, always placing one foot in front of the other.

This time, her thoughts just wouldn't seem to let go. The stream of others' doubts screaming in her mind, her situation questioning the truth in their judgments. *Is this where my battle ends?* The Woman's Home she wanted to create was once such an immensely strong conviction in her heart. Now, she couldn't even focus on it. Why did she feel so unsupported to create something she felt was so important and needed for hurt women from those who knew her? Did they feel it was a pipe dream? These thoughts fed her fears, keeping her from reaching out for help.

"And every day in every way, I am getting better and better." These words and Alex and Devon were all she really had right now in her life. As she sat looking at the fire, these thoughts were rapidly running through her head. She sat at the campground, her heart feeling like it was being split in half. She cried quietly, her heart searching for strength. *What do I really have right now? At this fire? In this campground? In my head...*

Sept 18th, 2010

As she sat there – with a pen in her hand and a notebook balanced on her knee – she felt as though someone was holding her hand and forcing her to write. She couldn't stop – her hand felt like it was latched onto the pen and the words flowed effortlessly.

They flowed from her heart onto paper. She paused for a minute and waited for the next words to come to her on their own. She suddenly realized that it had been exactly one month ago that day since she had reached her 'bottom.' Her absolute surrender to her situation. *Wow! How powerful,* she thought.

She put her pen back to the paper, and the words began to flow again.

She felt she couldn't explain it clearly enough. This wasn't something she could 'give' to anyone. She felt she couldn't 'make' people understand. It had to do with her heart, not her head.

Regardless, she continued to write; the words kept on flowing.

She thought of past conversations with those she cared about. "That is not what the Bible says," an old friend from the church she once belonged to pointed out. *I know,* she thought. She could only say the logic in the writings she had studied in the past weren't matching up with what she now knew in her heart.

She continued to write, and the words continued to flow onto the paper.

"That experience you described is exactly what it says in my Tantra book!" Another friend, one who claimed to be searching for answers, had told her. "Is it?" She had responded, "I don't know, I never read the book." She felt frustrated with the friend's reply, demonstrating her lack of understanding of what she was trying to explain. "You should read it," her friend had said. *Why? I am living it.* Her thoughts responded. She just couldn't seem to get anyone to understand what she was saying – that this was personal, not from a book.

"That is the ZEN!" A friend she knew was a practicing Buddha told her. She had to agree what she was feeling was definitely a connection through the quiet. *Hmm,* she thought. Probably the closest to what she felt.

"That is in 'Eat, Love, Pray'! She says that," another friend pointed out. She thought to herself, *how cool I am not crazy…*

The words continued to flow from her, out of her heart, onto paper.

She felt the clarity of her moment.

This was the start of the book.

~The Journey~

She hadn't set out for a Nomadic lifestyle when she ventured into this journey last year. Though as she sat there by the swamp, she could only feel redemption for the gift of the beauty before her. Thousands upon thousands of beautiful yellow butterflies filled the air. Infested almost, as the number was so vast, it felt threatening.

Moments like this, she thought to herself, are the moments I could thank the malevolent attitudes of those that couldn't understand my deviation from 'Corporate America.' At times over this last year the animosity from others felt like an inferno of hate waiting to consume her.

As she sat and sipped her coffee, feeling the sun on her face, listening to the harmonious sounds of nature, she knew this journey had led her here.

The book! It is time to write the book, she thought.

She no longer felt the exhaustion she felt hours before from the constant state of insomnia, keeping her awake at times in a state of neurosis as she struggled to find her footing for the next step.

It was time for her to capture all of these copious thoughts and redact her story. This story of survival when the world she once loved around her continued to exasperate her with its judgment. Her lack of willingness to retaliate against their attacks, knowing at some point the denouement would be such that she would find peace within herself.

As she choked back tears, the feeling was almost one of asphyxiation. The breath-taking view before her being the very thing she compared this journey to when she unintentionally set out on it last year. The sight before her mirroring the inextricable sensations she felt throughout her intestines, fluttering with anticipation.

Pulling out her pad and pen, she began to scribble. As her scribble turned to words and her words into sentences, she thought, how fortunate to be ambidextrous with so much to say.

The immaculate symbolism of rebirth as a new beginning in her life would no longer leave her feeling incapacitated by the judgment of others. She felt the freedom of life flashing before her as the words to express to others who desired to follow her path started to flow...

Chapter Three
~Time to Write~

She was sitting in her car, feeling her brain relax from the usual, constant barrage of thoughts that typically interrupted each other in her mind.

She didn't want to 'figure it out' today.

The day was starting to wake up, and the few cars that had been parked for the night around her had already started to come to life and leave to continue on with their travels.

She sat with her head back, eyes closed, on a pillow that was given to her by some new friends she had made when she had the last fiasco with her ex-husband. She laughed a bit to herself, remembering the conversation she had with them the previous night while sitting on their deck, enjoying a glass of wine and a bite to eat.

They had met a few times before the incident, though on the day she got in a fight with her ex-husband, and he threatened to call the police on her, she had gone over to their house to ask if she could use their phone to try and contact her children.

Funny how these things work out, she thought to herself, remembering how she had stayed long enough to let them see she really wasn't the psycho ex she seemed like, based on the escalated exchange between her and her ex-husband.

Her thoughts went to the news they gave her that he had in fact called the police, who in turn had told him he could do nothing if the neighbors had let her stay. That made her smile, thinking it must have been uncomfortable for him to see her car there last night. *Oh well,* she thought to herself.

Her day yesterday had been quite intense, though this was nothing new for her. The day had started out comparatively calm; she had felt connected to her core, at peace within herself, as she had walked by the stream and prayed. She had been focusing on staying calm, listening for guidance for future steps from her Creator.

One email exchange, a few lines of words, and I wonder all day about their meaning, she thought in frustration.

She could feel the sun coming in from the side window and a nice breeze flowing through the car. She listened to the sounds around her; the traffic on the nearby highway, the birds in the air.

She smiled to herself. She didn't mind sleeping in her car, as long as no one woke her up. The police around here were nosey and even when she was somewhere she was allowed to park overnight they still seemed to want to know why.

She closed her eyes again, her thoughts returning to the previous day.

After the email exchange, she seemed to have forgotten all about her trust in her Creator and her conviction that she wasn't going to let her own emotions be run by other people's opinions or words. She had felt anxious and unsure of what to do next.

She had sat in the library, hungry, feeling bad for herself because she had no money to get something to eat. She had forgotten that she had some food in the back of her car – one of those soup cups that just needs hot water poured into, as well as some cans of tuna. She had explored her options to see what she should do next.

Why am I not surprised my living expense check from school got screwed up? She thought.

This year had been like this. Every time she had thought she had figured out how she should move forward to stabilize her life again, something else happened to reassure her she was not in control. She had been humbled this year like never before in her life. She had remembered the concern from the gentleman she had bought her car from. He had offered her help if she needed it, and she had at the time refused because she had not needed any.

She wasn't comfortable asking people to help her, so she was very careful regarding whom she would accept help from. She had felt she could trust him since he was sincere, so even though she had declined at the time, she kept him in her mind for future reference.

She was not far from the location of his dealership, and she thought that he might be interested to learn more about the non-profit she had been creating over the last year. She decided to see if he would like to take her to lunch, where she could see if he had an interest in being involved with the non-profit's progress.

"Don't you think you should stop working on this non-profit and get a job so you can get a roof over your head?" George had asked her when she followed through and met with him. She felt her face flush, embarrassed. This happened a lot, each person forgetting she was putting forward her best efforts to do just that. It just seemed God had another plan for her.

"I am not really 'working' on the non-profit," she had said. "The writings just happen. I don't really think about writing as blocking me from anything."

He hadn't understood, and because of his judgment, she hadn't felt comfortable accepting lunch from him.

Well, at least I am getting better about asking for help, she thought to herself.

She opened her eyes and looked up at the sky. A flock of geese were flying overhead, and she watched the birds for a minute.

She closed her eyes again and thought of the women in the organization. She thought of Shania, and the connection Shania had helped her find the day before. She started to breathe, in through her nose, out through her mouth. Slowly.

She slowly started to pull down on her earlobes, concentrating on her breathing, thinking of Shania and wishing onto her a calm day with clarity in her mind. She knew Shania was having similar challenges and she knew how hard this year had been with no one seeming to understand the reality of her situation.

People seemed to all have solutions as to what she needed to do, and when she didn't feel their advice was the best option for her personally, they had walked out of her life. She prayed that Shania was able to persevere through those challenges of not having anyone physically in her life.

She thought of the other women in the group. She prayed through them in her mind, slowly breathing, while pulling slowly and gently on her earlobes.

Her thoughts returned to her friend. She said a prayer for him and his family.

Re-focus, she thought, *breathe.*

Her thoughts returned to the previous day. After leaving the dealership, she had felt the anxiety continuing to rise. She then made a decision to ask an elite friend of hers for help. It was so interesting to hear the response she had gotten. Once again, she thought about how people wanted to help on their own terms by telling her what she ought to do.

His offer last year had been left on the table and she had never regretted that. She had had lunch with him after her fishing trip and had shared with him where things were at, and he again reiterated he was there if she needed help. She had decided to ask if he would loan her gas money so she could get to school the following night, and perhaps see if he would like to take her to lunch.

She tried not to feel frustrated with his response. She knew his offer was sincere, though she also knew he had no understanding whatsoever of what she was trying to create for the non-profit.

"I have thought a lot about this," he had said. "I could give you monetary help, though that wouldn't help you long term. I believe everyone should work for every penny they earn, so if you want to work for me, we can discuss that," he said.

At first, this seemed like a great solution. Then she had remembered last year and their conversation back then, which was almost identical. He had expressed that if she worked for him, she needed to work full time and be 100% committed to his company. She had known when they spoke last year that her heart was not there, and this year, while she was working on her college degree and the non-profit, she didn't see having a tank of gas worth giving all she was working toward up.

Now, she took another deep breath. Today felt so calming to her. She had known peace throughout all the craziness this last year, though nothing felt as settling as this. She felt confident in her choice. This was new for her, she realized.

She felt as though her brain was being massaged. The calm in her chest and head was better than any time in the past when she had something to relax. Indeed, she felt relaxed to her core.

She laughed a bit at this, thinking how she had driven as far as she could last night to be close to school today so she could finish the portfolio for the non-profit and present it to the man she was hoping to be the head chair on its director's board.

She had slept in her car in a Walmart parking lot. In fact, she had actually slept very well.

She sat now, with her legs crossed out the driver's side car window, enjoying the quiet for a bit longer before she started to head the rest of the way to the school.

Her thoughts drifted back to her friend, and she said a prayer for him and his family. She went back to thinking over the last year and all the interactions she had with him.

She had initiated all of their correspondence. In the beginning, when he had first told her that he couldn't hurt his children, she had felt she understood. He was an amazing father, and through their friendship throughout the years, it was one of the things she respected about him. She had loved to listen to his stories about when he took his boys fishing, and she had been impressed that he was the cook in his family – even the fact he grew a garden and cooked from what he grew there.

She smiled when she thought of him because he had always made her laugh.

They had known each other for years, having been business acquaintances from a job long ago. He was not like most of the men she had known. He had never disrespected his wife in front of her, and he had never made any inappropriate advances either.

Throughout the years, he had always been someone whose intellect she had used to sort her head out, as his feedback was always honest and sincere, even if it wasn't what she wanted to hear. She thought of the time she had run into him and his wife years ago. She hadn't thought anything of it, though she remembered she was sincerely happy to see them, and also to meet his wife. Her thoughts moved forward to the shift in their friendship last year. She thought of how she had ended up in the hospital, feeling hopeless and seemingly unable to stop crying. She had so much to be happy for her in her life, and yet she had been having suicidal thoughts for months.

Upon coming out of the hospital, she had made some tough decisions career-wise. She decided to take a job for a company that paid less than what she was accustomed to, with the idea she could build a new career up and not have the stress that she thought was a factor to her sadness.

She recalled the email he had sent, asking how she was doing.

That was when it started; his name flashing across her email, giving her butterflies.

It continued like that for quite some time, and though she had known him for years, it seemed she suddenly couldn't receive enough of his words.

She sat up and got out of the car. She needed to get some clothes out of the back and think about where she was going to wash up. She opened the trunk. *Yikes, what a mess,* she thought to herself. She started to straighten it out, taking things out and reorganizing the trunk's contents.

I miss him so much, the thought abruptly popped in her head unwanted. She didn't want to miss him. She didn't want to think of how she felt when she was around him.

Throughout the year, she had been learning what it meant to respect him. Initially, she had thought that when his kids grew up, they would be together. Over this last year, she had come to realize that having that thought process was unfair to his wife. Her battle of surrender was constant as she learned every day more of what it was like to pull away.

He had never encouraged her to email and had, in fact, told her that he loved his wife and kids and could never hurt them. He had never talked disrespectfully about his wife and never alluded to anything more than the face value of where things with them were at.

She sighed. It had been a very long year for her.

She had finished organizing her trunk and had gotten back into the car to change. She was no longer self-conscious about how she looked, and she had become an expert at changing in the car without people driving by knowing what she was doing. Or maybe she didn't care anymore if someone drove by and saw her boobs. Regardless.

She felt her brain being massaged again, and she thought again of this newfound peace she was feeling.

She thought of how amazing God is. She thought of the insights he had given her yesterday into her own character.

She had always been a troubled child and had to leave her home when she was just 13. She thought of how the latest 'lesson' was so abundantly clear and quick to come to her.

She knew that she had been having separation anxiety about her friend that didn't need to be there. She had realized what she hoped this would be her final major imprint. Her desire to return home at 14 and the rejection of her parents not wanting her back had affected her. She had been given insight yesterday that her friend represented home to her because of the love he had taught her. She had been replaying his choice to remain with his family as a personal rejection toward her, not letting her return 'home.'

She recalled how quickly this had come to work itself out in her mind yesterday, as well as the peace that had immediately followed.

She got out of the car and put the pajamas she had been wearing into the trunk along with the rest of her belongings. She got back in and started her car up.

Time to write, she thought to herself.

~Some Mornings Just Happen~

Shaking. My back hurts. Cold. Chills. Once they start, it is hard to get them to stop.

Dammit, I lost my phone.

Back to sleep.

Wake up. *Damn, I am horny. I would so like a bed right now.*

Try not to freak about losing my phone.

I am a bit uncomfortable.

Back to sleep.

Tidal waves of panic at bay. *It's okay. I have plenty of time to find my phone. I can walk up to my friend's house and knock on his door. I am sure I can track him down and figure out where I left my phone. Well, I can call T-Mobile and tell them I lost my phone.*

Maybe they will have a way to get the numbers I called yesterday so I can reach the guy for the job interview today at 1. Thank goodness I planned that I wouldn't be back to NH until later in the day.

Maybe I can shower there as well. It's okay. Calm down.

Back to sleep.

Okay, so here is the plan. I am going to put my pants on… (Okay, well, I was under the blanket, and it did get a bit toasty in here.) Fold the blanket and put the blanket and pillow away. Walk up to my friend's house and ask if he has seen my phone. I will ask if his offer to shower there still stands.

That will give me plenty of time to figure out the next step.

Deep breathing. In through the nose, out through the mouth. Belly expanding with each inhale and contracting with each exhale.

Hmmm, this reminds me of another time I realized I had too much to drink, and I pulled over and slept it off. There would have been no way I could have driven last night after the bonfire, so regardless of my living situation, my sleeping arrangements last night would have been the same.

Oh look, there's my phone. Hmmm, now that changes everything.

Time to find an outlet to charge it.

Chapter Four
~Such an Ordinary Life~

So average, so unique, all the same,

A lawn to mow, a child to address, a bed to sleep, a body to hold,

American dream,

So living the achievements,

Of a life hard-earned.

Such an ordinary life,

Oh, so average, so unique, all the same,

Coffee to brew, cocktails to make, barbi to grill, Houseguests to entertain,

So average, oh so unique all the same.

Such an ordinary life,

Really the alarms go off, kids to feed, school scurry,

Same roads to travel,

Same people to see,

Such an ordinary life I have built around me.

Accomplishments,

New levels to dream of,

Life surrounding me, once content,

DANA VILANDRE

Now unrest, not what is seen,
So proud to be the king,
Of the domain I call my home,
The world I have built around me,
My kingdom, not mine alone.
My eyes are now wide open,
Though at times I feel blind is what I was meant to be,
This ordinary life,
Contentment in memories I never needed to see.

~Somedays~

Somedays, I am drowning in my reality to find myself lost in tears of my misunderstood perception.

Somedays, I am looking for the point when my yang can meet my yin and become a mesh of comprehension and humility. Not jagged edges cutting into my recognition because of my lack of both.

Somedays, I think I am a human science experiment. And I seriously hope the foretelling of my future does not have anything to do with what I see happen to frogs…

Chapter Five
~Defining Mr. Right~

Her days were always so interesting. *To honestly keep someone up with all that had happened in the past twenty-four hours would be a full-time job alone,* she thought to herself.

The last few days had been intense for her. She was sitting in her friend's driveway by the beach house she was so fortunate to be able to stay at for a short period. Her mind thought of the events that happened so rapidly as of late. She had met a former first officer for the US Air Force – a Gulf War veteran. Two purple hearts. He had played one inning in one game for a major sports team that won a world series.

He was even a massage therapist! He was an attractive, funny writer and currently the personal assistant to one of the local proprietors in town. They had a whirlwind of time together. He had been 'exploring' himself the last few years after what was to be a final horrific breaking point in his life, which sometimes happens to a person. He hadn't been in a relationship with a woman in three years since, and to him, she was amazing.

Their chemistry was like a flame! BAM! Energy through the roof and an honesty and openness that skyrocketed their relationship quickly.

I am totally ruined when it comes to dating, she thought to herself.

She didn't want a mindless connect, though if she did find a mindless connect, she wanted it as just that. Mindless. And if the mindless had a problem with any part of her, she was willing to walk on past them. She was open and honest with people, and if she wasn't going to get that behavior in return, she was fine with moving on. She no longer felt the need to conform from what she felt was right for her in her life for another person.

She said a prayer, her emotions confused over the last few days' events. She was truly sincere about her feelings for Mike. He was amazing. She had thought in her mind that perhaps maybe this was her Creator's way of helping her to move her heart away from her friend.

She felt that stab in her chest as she recalled the struggles she had in her heart and mind as soon as she was away from Mike, her thoughts continually thinking of her friend.

I feel like I am speed dating, she muttered under her breath as she tried to refocus away from how her friend and his wife were spending the holiday.

Yes, I do have a mental checklist with men now, she remarked to herself. She thought on for a minute. *Was this okay to even have?* She wondered. This made her think of the choices she had made in her life.

Yes, I think this is a very good thing, she reassured herself.

She thought of the circumstances that had led up to her present meeting with Mike. It was most certainly like magic; this game that she continued to play with God. It was like a game of red-light green-light.

She found herself faced with some incredibly challenging situations this past year and she had been learning to trust the answers to her prayers. She knew in her heart she was doing the best she could with her core being. Sometimes, these situations had led her into scarier ones, though when she would come through them with integrity, she always felt God blessed her for respecting him the best way she knew how. She had been out on a date with a man she had met at a local bar. It had been a long time since she had a male company in the romantic sense – well, at least for her anyway. And she had met someone local that she enjoyed talking with. She had been out on a third date with him when 'the' conversation inevitably started.

"Joe says that if you are hanging out with me, and I am smoking you up and buying you beers, you should be taking care of me." They had been sitting on his deck, listening to some classic rock and enjoying the sun. Or so she had thought.

This was an interesting train of thought for her, and being the study of men that she was, she was curious to know more. "Oh, really? Interesting. So, what is Joe's girlfriend like?" she asked.

"He doesn't have one," he replied, not seeming to notice the irony in his words.

She had let the conversation shift as a song he enjoyed came on. *"Hey, put this bandana on!"* He went into his foyer and took a bandana off the mirror and came out and handed it to her. She enjoyed his silliness and gladly took the bandana and put it on. She began dancing around to some old classic rock, being totally silly.

"I feel like I am hanging out with my sister," he commented.

"Now, that isn't a bad thing, is it?" She asked. She enjoyed laughing and having fun. She kept her temper in check as she remembered the way this conversation went last time – frustrating for her. He seemed to say the right things that said he understood, though they kept coming back to this.

"I really like you," he said. "I just like to have sex with one person while I am dating." She had felt her frustration rise again and had said another prayer.

"Why do we have to discuss if we are going to have sex? Why can't we just enjoy each other's company?" she had asked and had gotten up to go into the house to use the bathroom.

She smiled now, remembering the next set of events. The magic, so to say. She realized that if she had not had sex with her friend, even when they had so many opportunities, and continued respecting each other, why would she even entertain it with this man who was already making her feel bad for not having it?

When she had come out of the bathroom, Mark had handed her a sculpture of a lion.

Throughout the year, she had come to compare men in her life to animals. She called it the Kingdom. There were elephants, roosters, horses, teddy bears, and most of all, lions. To be a lion in her Kingdom, a man had to be pretty darn special.

Poor Mark, she thought to herself. He had no idea she had this analogy, and that he in no way classified as a lion. To her, this was a sign that she did need to leave.

Nonetheless, she left quickly after that exchange, and as nicely as she could. She walked up to the beach. The sun was dimmed and the clouds that showered warm rain sporadically were darkening the sky slightly. It was still early, and she had felt like being out for a bit. She sat on a bench and put her head back and closed her eyes.

Her thoughts went back to her friend. She had learned so much through just her thoughts of him. Furthermore, he was incredibly respectful of her. She said a prayer for him and his family. She missed him and felt the familiar ache of surrender. That's when she realized she was crying.

No sense sitting here crying, she thought. She got up and started to walk along the strip.

She had a couple of dollars in her pocket, which was unusual for her. She decided to see if a local haunt had cheap drafts and she would work on some writing.

That was when Mike walked in.

She got up off the blanket she had been sitting on, her mind quickly reviewing the time she'd spent with Mike. They had danced on the beach under the stars. They had sat and talked for hours on end until late into the night. They had such a strong intensity between them that they both knew sex was a very small aspect of their relationship.

For the first time in a long time, she hadn't had the constant thoughts of her friend alongside her.

She sighed. She did feel slightly broken today. She went from no men in her life to speed dating through some pretty spectacular men in a very short span of time. They had all been quite interesting and amazing in their own respective ways. She had enjoyed different aspects about them, although in each case, when she tried to express thoughts that were contrary to what they believed in, she couldn't seem to communicate with them at all. It always seemed to escalate into something deeply uncomfortable for her personally. She tried to talk it through each time, though they weren't even willing to hear her point of view, let alone respect it. So, she had felt she needed to move on.

Above all, I want to date a man who loves and respects God as I do, she thought to herself. Her mind drifted back to her friend. She thought of the conversation she had with him last year when she first realized she was seeing signs from her Creator for the direction she was meant to walk.

"You should be careful who you tell this to," he had remarked to her, "Everyone will think you are crazy."

~Assholeness~

So, you meet someone, and maybe they are an asshole. Okay, so you give them the benefit of the doubt that perhaps they are just having a bad day and don't realize how loudly their asshole side is showing at the moment.

So, you kindly or jokingly make light of their assholeness. Maybe then, at that point, they realize either that 1) they were being an asshole, or 2) you are way too sensitive. Either way, the assholeness should subside. Albeit there are cases when people are plain old assholes...

Some are just blind to this side of themselves, and then perhaps they become 'enlightened' once it's pointed out. And maybe some could use some discipline and maybe a sting to the ego, which would in turn set in motion an internal need for change.

And some will just remain assholes because their end objective or focus is their utmost priority, and honestly, if there are feelings hurt along the way... well, so be it.

At this point, it is up to you how you deal with it.

"That is just how I am. I treat everyone like that!" At some point this last year, I realized I was no longer going to be "everyone."

I have no room in my life for bullshit, insincerity, ugliness in attitudes, fighting, animosity, or anger. I do not have any need to want or need what is not mine. I do not hang out with people who do not allow me to feel good about myself and the negative response they trigger in me when I am around them. I do not need this anymore.

I am cool just to be me.

I will not allow anyone to treat me in a way I would not treat someone else.

Treat people with respect, treat people with kindness, and treat people with sincerity,

...and if someone you know has this disease of 'Assholeness,' know that it is not contagious. Well, not if you are immune to it. Let them own their own part in the play...

Chapter Six
~One Summer Day~

She felt her heart racing as she searched her brain to figure out what day it was.

Okay, it is Tuesday, she thought, feeling the relief relax her shoulders. *I start classes again tomorrow.*

She went back to her writings. Well, if someone was to call them that.

It was July 5th. She was sitting outside of her friend's condo on a blanket in his driveway.

Her hands were doodling in her notebook, though her thoughts were elsewhere. She recalled her decision not to contact Mike last night to follow through with the plans he had made for them with his best friends.

Then, her thoughts directed to her friend. She had a flash of guilt travel through her chest. *Am I relieved to see Mike go?* She thought to herself.

She stood for a minute and stretched, her face toward the sky and arms wide. She focused her attention on God and started to pray, refocusing her thoughts away from her friend. She would have liked nothing more than to sit and daydream about him, however, she had committed to herself that she would not covet what wasn't hers to desire.

Soon, she started her 'game' with God. She always tried to think of new fun ways to describe God and their relationship in her 'game.'

Our Father, most Awesomeness of Storytellers, Guider, she prayed in her head. "How Holy is your name, I cannot even begin to say it enough."

This made her smile. She wished she could explain to someone these moments of peace. She had tried many times, but people didn't understand. They kept calling her crazy or pitying her. She tried to explain she didn't need anything from them, just a friend to talk to, but people didn't like what she had to talk about. As a result, many of them no longer answered her calls.

She sighed and sat back on the blanket, cross-legged. She stretched again, taking a deep breath and focusing on relaxing her shoulders from the stress she had felt built up in them. Her thoughts returned to Mike and the events that happened yesterday morning.

They had been having such an amazing time together. They talked late into the night under the stars, and they danced on the beach in the moonlight. They took long walks and talked about life and laughed at silly things. She loved how spontaneous he was, and they experienced some amazingly cool things in a very short span of time together.

For the first time in a very long time, she hadn't had that ache thrum in her heart when she thought of her friend.

She had respected who Mike was and had understood him at a deeper level. She even understood the out-of-the-norm choices that he had made due to heartache in the last couple of years. She sighed again and then returned to her game.

God, please help me to stay focused on you, and away from men, she said this prayer frequently, even though she seemed to forget it when the next man came along, striking her fancy. Lately, it seemed like even though she had such a strict checklist, roosters seemed to keep sneaking through, disguised as Mr. Fabulous.

Thy Kingdom come... she continued with her prayer, refocusing her thoughts. She didn't want to go back down that road again. It always inevitably led to her friend, and her memories would turn to desire with just a few moments of indulgence.

She said a quick prayer for him and his family, praying for them to be happy and healthy.

She prayed for her children. Leaning forward onto the blanket with her arms stretched out before her, she thought of her kids and a recent conversation she had with them.

"Mom," Devon had asked in her little guess-what voice, "Alex beat up a boy at school."

They had been driving to grab a couple of subs and hang out for a bit. Upon hearing this, she had looked over at Alex sitting next to her. He hadn't seemed too worried. She was wondering in her head if this was going to end up being one of those mom-witch moments when Devon added more details to the story.

"A kid called a girl fat, and Alex beat him up."

Now, Devon and Alex went to different schools. Part of her had felt impressed that the news of the fight went through two schools, and another part of her had been impressed her son had stuck up for a girl. She searched for the part of her that felt bad her son beat up a kid at school.

"I didn't beat him up," Alex had said, "I just shoved him. Mom. It was Shawn. You know."

She recalled a few conversations he had shared with her about Shawn. The consensus between them had already formed that Shawn was an imbecile with no social skills.

Now, she smiled to herself as she sat on the blanket. She had not been sure what was the best way to respond, so she had said what was on her mind. "So umm, this isn't going to be some new thing with you, is it? Are you going to start getting in fights now?"

Alex had just rolled his eyes. Her kids were used to her talk.

She closed her eyes, trying to calm her mind and heart so she could focus on her prayer.

This year had been about trusting these prayers she was confident were being heard. She didn't know for sure – after all, how could anyone? She recalled how amazing things felt when she handled an unexpected situation in a way she felt absolutely certain about.

Yes, they are being heard, she thought to herself.

On Earth, as it is in Heaven, she thought to herself.

Then, she considered how she always forgot that not everyone was nice. She felt a flush of embarrassment, recalling how someone had recently made her feel bad for sharing with them that she had fallen on hard times. She took a deep breath and recited a quick prayer. This train of thought led her to Bill, and she had a prayer for him and the company he worked for, too.

I feel like I just went through this with him. Oh, wait I did. With this, her thoughts returned to Mike and the intensity of them discussing something that was hurtful to her, which ended with him storming out of the room. Her experience had been similar with Bill. There had been lot of intensity between them. She had quickly realized the differences were so vast between them that they were major fight escalators.

She prayed for her tongue and for her to have more discipline and control over who she shares her life with.

With that, she returned to her game. *Give us this day our daily bread,* she prayed.

She took a deep breath as she felt the calm come over her chest and shoulders. Even though her friend's condo was not right next to the ocean, she could smell the sea in the air. She said a quick prayer of gratitude that she had Jesse and his boyfriend in her life. She was so deeply grateful that Jesse was local for a few months, staying at his dad's condo. He had not hesitated in opening his futon up for her.

She felt so fortunate to be right near the ocean, where she was able to take long walks along the beach, praying and asking for guidance in her situation.

Forgive us our trespasses... she thought of the conversation she had with Mike about Jesse's mom. She knew the story she told him was one the woman herself would have shared, though she certainly felt it wasn't cool of her to share it on her behalf. She thought of all the times she posted about oversharing, and it wasn't nice. She made a mental note to talk to her about it if their paths were to cross again. She had already told Mike she felt like it wasn't her story to tell. She searched her heart to see if there were any other blockers.

As we forgive those that trespass against us. She thought again of Mike. Was she being unreasonable? Was she holding on to something she needed to apologize for?

Her thoughts drifted back to yesterday morning. "Anyone who is real with themselves would admit that!" He had yelled at her in a voice that certainly told her he thought she was oblivious.

"I am not saying there are not people who have had it worse than you or I have, I am just saying I don't feel it is up to another person to decide someone else's level of pain," she explained. "I built an organization based on just that."

He had stormed out of the condo, saying something about how she could call him.

Or not, she thought now to herself, sitting on the blanket.

She thought once again about her friend. She had never wanted him to feel bad about his decision not to see her intentionally. She thought now of how she realized how hurt she had been, even though she had understood it was the right decision. Knowing that, she said a prayer for him and his wife and their family.

For thine is the Kingdom, The power and the glory forever. Amen.

She stood up and walked over to the table and picked up her coffee, which she had been sipping on for the last couple of hours.

She knew she was still holding on to her friend in her heart. She felt raw and open before God. She stood there for a minute, cup in her hands, eyes closed, her face to the sky, and took another deep breath.

As she exhaled, her thoughts now went to the week ahead and her next game plan to reestablish her life.

Suddenly, with a lurch of her stomach, she recalled that she had switched nights for her classes. Today was the first day they were starting back up. *I am such an airhead,* she thought to herself as she looked at the time on her phone. She realized her classes started in an hour and she still had to get dressed.

Time to go, she thought to herself as she picked up her blanket. *Time to go.*

Words… Are Just Experience with A Meaning Defining Them

Everything is so significant in life.
Or is it?
Everywhere there are signs when living the sincerest paths possible.
Or are there?
Everyday solidifies your personal truth when connected to your core.
Or does it?
Everyone that comes into your path comes into it for a purpose.
Or do they?
Define…
Faith.
Define…
Kindness.
Define…
Respect.
Define…
Truth.
Define…
Forgiveness…

Chapter Seven
~Friendships~

She sat on the dock, listening to the waves as they lightly came upon the bank. *What an amazing day,* she thought to herself.

She was half-listening to the kids play in the lake next to her. They had visited this spot last weekend, and with time on her side, the kids had asked her if they could go there today since they had Rob and Hannah with them.

She stretched her shoulders and took a deep breath. *It feels so nice to take a breath for pleasure instead of to calm myself,* she thought to herself.

Her thoughts went to the events of the last few days, and the array of emotions she had experienced. All that made her realize the point she personally had come to with the relationships she had in her life hitherto.

God is Amazing! She thought to herself. She had always felt this way, even as a child, and it felt nice to be able to feel the experience freely. She sat there, her heart brimming with peace. The sensations she felt throughout her body were like nothing she had ever experienced before.

I wish I could explain it clearly, she thought. This wasn't the first time she had felt this urgency to share this with other people – even though every time it seemed to get more intense.

It seemed to her that every time she trusted her core and stayed committed to her convictions, the serenity and absolute joy she felt were like nothing she had ever experienced in the past.

Love is addicting, she thought, *Way better than drugs.* She smiled to herself, thinking of her enjoying wine and Scooby snacks. She felt pretty good about this.

She looked over at the kids. Hannah had climbed up a tree the others had been jumping off into the lake from. She was now standing on the branch, afraid to jump into the water.

She listened to the kid's conversations, and for the most part, she was pleased with what she heard. She smiled to herself, feeling as though her soul had been bear-hugged.

She felt truly blessed to have such cool kids. She always enjoyed spending time with them, even when Alex, the oldest, was complaining.

Devon was saying encouraging things to help Hannah muster up the courage to jump. She was so proud of the way her daughter loved her friends.

Alex suggested Hannah sing a song in her head.

"Alex, that works for you. She has to figure out what works for her," Rob answered. Tingles went down her spine as she thought of how cool the signs were from God when she was staying close to Him. Rob's response to Hannah's situation was exactly how she felt about life.

How funny God is, she thought, and this weekend was exactly that.

She stood up and walked around a bit, stretching her arms up and concentrating on relaxing her chest.

She had fallen on some hard times this last year, and she had made a lot of decisions that went against common belief.

Faith. This single word came to her mind.

She heard the splash as she began to register the fact that Hannah had jumped. She came out of her reverie, focusing on the kids so they could feel her love. She had such a horrible memory and she often was sidetracked mid-sentence.

Hannah came up out of the water, yelling, "Oh My God! That was so scary! I have the worst wedgie!"

She laughed out loud. Hannah's response to the jump was the opposite of how everyone else had reacted. Hannah had not thought it 'fun.'

She felt her brain relax a bit.

Wow! she thought, *we would not even be having this experience.*

She loved how free her children were to explore fun on their own.

Her thoughts went to yesterday morning, and an interaction she had with someone who had been one of her closest friends. The plan had been to stay with Sarah and her husband that weekend so she could spend time with her children.

She had felt so hurt with the exchange. She recalled the conversation she had with her kids when she read them what she had written about being out fishing. Her kids had been quiet, and she had known Sarah was sitting in her kitchen listening through the window. This has come right after Sarah had said she was ruining her daughter's life because of her own example and history with men.

She had tried to remain calm. She had struggled with men her whole life and she didn't want to pass this onto her daughter.

She had gone out onto Sarah's porch with her notebook. She had bowed her head, praying for her mind to calm down. *Please God,* she thought, *I don't want to ruin my daughter.*

She thought of how Sarah had asked if she had slept with Mike, and she'd been taken aback. What does that have to do with anything?

She had felt cut to her core as she sat and prayed, and she had realized she could no longer stay at Sarah's house overnight.

She felt the anxiety throughout her chest. She had been able fortunate to find a place to stay every time she had her children with her, and this was the first time she didn't have anywhere to go.

This made her think of her car. She had finally had a bit of gas in the tank, but then the transmission had messed up the night before. She hadn't been able to work on the boat today out of fear of being stranded out there with the car. She hadn't thought through how she was going to deal with that situation, though that now seemed minor compared to not having a place to take her children to stay.

She recalled Sarah's words, "You claim to love God and believe the Bible, and you won't even look at your own behavior." She had felt stung by what she said. Sarah had continued, "Zack and I have agonized over this constantly. We do not know how to help you."

She had calmly tried to explain her point of view, but Sarah started throwing up different men in her face, including James. She felt like she was going to throw up.

"I have prayed and asked my kids forgiveness for that decision," she admitted.

She was brought out of her thoughts by Devon. "Mom, Mom, watch me!" It had been the third time Devon had wanted her to watch her jump from the tree. She laughed, "Devon, I already know what it looks like to watch you jump out of the tree."

She leaned back on her elbows, her face toward the skies, eyes closed, the sun beating down just right.

She felt so taken care of.

Her thoughts went back to her discussion with Sarah. "I am the only friend you have left!" Sarah had yelled at her.

Instantly she had felt ashamed. It was true. The women she had been a friend with up to that point were no longer in her life. She recalled the different conversations with the two people that she had considered herself closest to, and in the moment of intensity from the emotions elicited through Sarah's words, she had forgotten these women were not women she would seek to have in her life today.

She had worked hard this last year not to inconvenience those around her. She had worked hard at staying upbeat, especially around her kids, and only shared the more intense moments with a select group of persons. Sarah had been one of them. She stood and stretched again; her arms extended high to the sky so she could release some of the stress knots she felt cramping in her back.

Sarah's words came back to her to haunt her once again. "You always have a different man. You are being a bad role model for Devon."

She remembered how before she had married her husband, she had decided not long into her engagement with him that she was making a mistake and had returned the ring back to him. They had a dinner date with Sarah and Sarah's first husband which had already been planned, and she had decided they should still go. In her mind, she always wanted to remain friends with the men she dated. She felt she had enjoyed their company and not being a 'couple' shouldn't change that.

However, she recalled Sarah's reaction that night when she had finally gotten a moment alone as they were cleaning up the dinner dishes.

"You are making a massive mistake," she had said, "He is good for you and keeps you away from all these men."

She didn't blame Sarah for her failed marriage, and she hadn't listened to her that day anyway. It was her own jealousy that had prompted her to reconsider, but now, as she thought of the conversation she'd had just yesterday, she realized that in Sarah's mind, she needed a 'man' to settle down with to fix her so she could find God. Interesting, it would be a man that would set her straight and help her find God – though, not in the physical aspect. It was her love for him that she found her Creator.

Now, as she sat by the lake with her children, she thought of the cute police sergeant she had met just last weekend. He was single and very handsome. He had moved into a house behind an old friend of hers whom she often visited here in Holbrooke.

They had all sat and talked long into the night about life on her friend's porch her last visit here. The physical pull was strong, though she no longer based this feeling or physical appearance as a reason to jump into a relationship. Plus, they had one MAJOR difference of opinion, and she knew immediately she would not compromise either of their integrity.

She thought of him for a moment. He had texted her and asked if she was going to come to Holbrooke. She had said she didn't believe so, and a thought crossed her mind on how he would feel if drove by and saw her car here? She realized it didn't matter, and she had no reason to update him on her change of plans. She didn't want to lead the friendship into a path she wasn't willing to walk herself.

She sat back on the dock, from where she could see a boat was sailing by with a dog standing on the bow. She thought this was funny and called out to the kids, "Hey, look at the dog." They all stopped and looked, and after laughing for a bit, they went back to playing.

She loved listening to her daughter's laughter. She leaned back and closed her eyes, thinking, *God, thank you.* She felt the gratitude for the moment to her core.

"Mom, when are we leaving?" Alex soon called over to her.

"Whenever you want." she answered. There were some perks to having no physical obligations to be at.

"Can we go now? I am starting to get hungry," Alex asked. A stream of 'me too' followed from the others.

"Sure!" She stood up again and grabbed her book bag.

"Mom! Mom! One more time. Watch me jump!" It was Devon. She smiled. It was the fourth time she had yelled for her to watch.

She loved watching her children enjoy being kids. She recalled Alex and Rob earlier that morning sitting on the deck of the friend's home they ended up being able to stay at the night before. The deck overlooked the lake, and she sat and watched Alex and Rob playing Uno and talking quietly to one another. Her heart had filled with joy upon seeing this.

Funny how it all seems to work out, she thought to herself. She knew it was God.

It was time to go. She took another look around her. She smiled and breathed in the fresh air.

The kids were leaving their names on an already well-autographed step nailed to the 'jumping' tree.

She thought of their left memory. She thought of their future, and she smiled again.

She felt a calmness befall her, which was even deeper than what she had experienced all day. She turned and started up the path.

She said a prayer of gratitude because she knew to her core that what she was teaching her kids mattered the most.

~A Piece of Glass~

I looked in the mirror today. What did I see?
A forty-year-old woman. Even though I was alone,
I didn't recognize her as me.
Her chin seemed to sag, her eyes bloodshot and tired,
Maybe it was last night's whine,
Maybe it was feeling the drain of saying goodbye to what was desired.
I looked away quickly, as though embarrassed and shy.
Though I was alone in the room, I didn't think to ask my brain why.
The woman looking back wasn't who I was hoping to see.
The look was all wrong, not who I pictured her to be.
That piece of glass, that mirrored image I saw, didn't seem to reflect.
The love and the laughter I wanted others to feel. Instead looking back, I felt neglect.
The lines on my face appearing deep in the light,
And the sleepless nights of worry, not telling a story of winning the fight.
Does the image reflected hold so much control on my mind?

And if I don't have someone on my cheer team, will the internal peace be mine to find?

Chapter Eight
~Let Live. Let's Love~

She sat and listened to him talk.

"You know, I am their running back. It's all I do, you know." He went on and on with the story of how he was the star of his school football team.

She listened to him, wondering why he was lying to her. She had known him for a couple of years now, and she knew his family. She knew he didn't play for his school football team, and she knew he rarely went to school.

As she listened to him, she thought of her own teen years, and wondered what adults had thought of her when she made up a story on why she was sleeping on their couch and not with her family.

She had gotten in a lot of trouble before she was even officially a teenager, so it wasn't really a surprise when she had progressed to the point of stealing a car when she was barely into her teens. The incident led her to be sent away from her family at quite a young age.

She had lived a street life, making decisions to do what

she needed to do to survive. She partied hard with no restrictions, and even though she had found herself in some very scary situations, she always seemed to get herself out of them unscathed. Well, unscathed externally at least. Internally, things wouldn't play out for years to come.

Yeah, not until I turned forty, she thought to herself, thinking of the choices she had been faced with this past year.

She refocused her thoughts on Timmy. She always felt like she was being a bitch to him. She thought of this now as he was going on with his story and thought maybe her impatience with him was because he reminded her of herself at his age. He was incredibly intelligent, and she felt he could be making better choices.

He had a hard home life, and she knew of it. She had listened to the screaming and anger through the thin walls when her brother had lived next to him. She still felt frustrated that he would always be over here smoking cigarettes he couldn't afford and getting high.

She decided not to call him out on his obvious lies. Her brother's roommate's younger brother was over, and she thought maybe Timmy was trying to impress him.

Who am I to judge? She thought to herself.

She asked Timmy instead if he had started looking into colleges.

He smirked at her a bit, finished his cigarette, and went into the apartment.

She knew he hated it when he saw her car parked outside when he was coming over. She had a way of calling him out on his behaviors that he couldn't quite figure out how to dodge.

She considered asking the roommate's younger brother what was going on in his life when she realized she didn't really care. She sat back on the couch, picking up her notebook.

The couch stunk, but she tried not to think about it. She had put a sheet on it last time she was here, though they mixed up the concept and moved the sheet to cover the part to sit on instead of the area to rest one's head.

She closed her eyes and bit her tongue. She really didn't want to be a bitch; it was just this place brought out her worst. She sat there for a bit, thinking of their decision to stay here last night. Her kids got along well with her brother, though she could personally only handle him in small doses. She and her children decided they would stay over instead of traveling all the way to the campground where they were going to stay at. She did enjoy spending time with her brother's roommate and his girl, and her brother had started dating a teacher, so he was more tolerable lately.

Her brother had a degenerative disease that somehow prevented him from having 'filters' in his thought process. With no effort whatsoever to control his tongue, he was more than a bit challenging for her to deal with. Hanging out with him was difficult for her, and she hated to feel that she was using his place because it was convenient. She had long ago stopped giving him her opinion as it always led to a fight and him throwing her out. Now, she just sat there and kept her mouth shut.

Probably why I always fall asleep out here, she thought. A shudder ran through her as she thought of how nasty the couch was. In fact, the whole city was nasty, but that is just what it was like here in Fitzdale.

She recalled the last time they had stopped here when they were coming back from Holbrooke. Within the first half an hour of being there she had been informed of three arrests just in the small area they were staying in. The first was a murderer who had shot a store clerk in the head for a bag that he thought had money in it, even though it had only contained the clerk's dinner. The second was a pedophile, who was her brother's roommate's girl's best friend's grandfather. The third was a seize on a friend's cannabis supply.

She remembered how mad she was last year when her ex-husband had told her he didn't want her kids to visit her here. He thought it wasn't safe.

She sighed and sat back up to write in her notebook. She figured there must be a story with all this somewhere.

She thought of her brother's roommate and smiled because she had a strong feeling that God brought him into her brother's life. He was an ex-con, albeit the type that paid his dues to society and was just trying to do the right thing. She enjoyed his honesty and knew he was genuine. She thought him a good influence for her brother.

She had been listening to her brother's woes for years and was acutely aware of what conversations were fight-escalators between her and him.

Which would be all of them, she thought to herself.

Her daughter came out of her brother's home and climbed on her lap. She shifted to put the notebook down and enjoy her thirteen-year-old snuggling into her like a baby.

She breathed in her daughter's freshly shampooed hair and they sat there for a bit, the surroundings no longer mattering. She said a prayer of gratitude for being able to be a mom.

She thought about the choices she had made over the years. Even though she admitted that some of them really sucked, and that maybe she was a little too intense with the specific knowledge she fed her kids. She knew her children were aware her advice wasn't coming from some random magazine or child-rearing book, but instead from experience and love.

She knew that despite this, she couldn't predict the exact circumstances her kids would end up in. However, since she was always teaching them to follow their core, because of this, she had to trust their choices. Regardless, they seemed far too young to make those choices right now.

She took a deep breath and took in the scent of her daughter, praying she could continue to guide her little girl to always make the choices best for her.

~Transference~

Frustrated words, shortened fuse. You have an attitude; I am less than amused.

You are hitting an age I would like to undo; one I wish I had a map on how to get through.

I wish I could light up your path with golden bricks where you should walk.

Feed you some telepathic vibes on how to correct your talk.

Protect you through the alleyways, carry you on the painful days.

I am sure I seem harsh and you say I go overboard.

If I didn't feel it was so important, I wouldn't fight with you to be heard.

I once loved to have fun, too. Hang with my girlfriends, listen to music, played with toys.

Though I wish I had made better choices and was less destructive when it came to boys.

Take time to figure them out, see what type of boy they really are.

It was hard to date the boys who today would rather hang at a bar.

Learn about romance and silly fun dates,

Keep clothes on a bit longer.

GYPSY NOMAD HIPPIE CHICK

Look for soulmates.
Life has been lived through eyes educated by pain…
Hmmm…
Okay, so the topic of men had nothing to do
With the fact you didn't bring a change of clothes with you..

Chapter Nine
~Resolve~

She sat on the hood of her car, staring out over the small pond. It was quite picturesque, with a layer of algae collecting on the top, blending with the reflection of the trees and the lily pads.

For the first time in days, it was not raining. The sun was out. The weather was perfect. It was one of those days when the breeze was just right, and the temperature was how one wished every day was.

She took a deep breath, feeling at peace and calm. She didn't have to be at work for another hour, and she was happy to be able to have some time to pray and focus her mind on the day ahead.

She could hear the nearby traffic from the highway. The pond was not far just off a highway exit, and although it was the image of tranquility, the real world was only a tree line away.

She sat alone for a bit, looking over the pond. Her thoughts went to thinking of a girlfriend of hers who had thrown herself into the pond a few years back in a state of hopelessness. She thought of that and the other incidences that had led her to starting the organization for women she had been creating. She understood her girlfriend's actions. Perceived love can make a woman do crazy things.

She knew. She was the queen of crazy.

She smiled at this thought and jumped off the car, stretching her tense limbs. Sighing, she walked over to the edge of the pond. Standing there, hands on her hips, head back and eyes closed, she was deep in thought – in prayer.

Her mind traveled back to the conversation she had with Mike last night.

She had decided to get in touch with him the night before for some Scoobie snacks. She knew that regardless of how he perceived their relationship, he completely understood the concept of relaxing the mind with some Scoobie Doo.

"If you want to come by after you get out of school tonight, I will have some. I'll buy you a beer at the Tavern," he had texted her.

She had thought for a bit about this. She hadn't seen him since she had left his house in anger, after which she finally realized their communication was not happening. She had only had a brief interaction with him since, which was by text about borrowing his can opener. She smiled as she thought of it now. Her banter with her exes always made her smile.

She felt the sun's rays on her face and was enjoying the peace of the moment. She was oblivious to the walkers that were coming and going along the bike path right next to the pond. Indeed, she was in her own world.

"Good morning, God!" She said aloud as she stretched her hands out and felt her chest expand.

She opened her eyes and started walking along the edge of the pond.

She thought again of her girlfriend, and the string of events over the past few years ever since she'd dated that boyfriend from hell.

Her thoughts returned to Mike and the night before. She had forgotten so quickly how easy he was to talk to. Well, when it wasn't something he disagreed with anyway. She smiled now as she recalled the conversation that had sparked as soon as she had arrived at his place last night.

She had sat on chair in his room, waiting for him to finish getting ready to go out to the tavern. She had felt the energy between them, and though it wasn't totally uncomfortable, she hadn't wanted to mislead him either.

"I just want to be sure you understand I am being honest and upfront with you," she had said. "I do not want to mislead you about us in any way. I just want to stay friends."

"Since when do you hold anything back in what you say to me?" He had asked with a laugh. He had then gone on to talk about how many days they had known each other, and how he felt their relationship was much more than any single moment in time.

She had sat there for a minute listening to him, that familiar tug that told her he thought she just needed to let go of her friend in her heart and give their relationship a chance.

Nonetheless, it was a conversation they had had in the past.

She had thought through this while he babbled on, smiling and listening. She was admiring his features and the sound of his voice as he talked.

She had searched her heart often since she had walked out of his place that last moment. She really enjoyed spending time with him, and they had incredibly intense interactions for a few weeks. What they had felt for each other was very real and fervent for them both. However, she had come to realize she really was all set to be just his friend.

She thought now of how refreshing it was to be able to talk to a man and be completely honest.

"Okay, so you just used a whole lot of words to say a whole heck of a lot of nothing," she had said and dramatically jumped off the chair. "Let's go get some beers!"

She smiled up at him to lighten the moment.

"Wow, I forgot about that smile," he had said, looking a bit frustrated that she had made light of his professed feelings.

"Listen, really," she had said. "I enjoy your company very much. I just do not want to revisit the romantic side of what we had. I just think our issues with communication are too frustrating for me personally."

They had proceeded to go out to the tavern and have a few drinks. Mike was a talented writer, and she read him a few of her latest stories. His critique was good, though she wasn't sure how he felt about her stories personally, especially the ones which he was mentioned. She didn't care. She hadn't written them for him.

She sighed now, recalling how at the end of the night she had still needed to reiterate that regardless of her feelings for her friend, she and Mike were not meant to be a couple.

She walked back over to her car, feeling good about how she had handled the situation last night. She bent in through the window so she could glance at her phone. *Another 15 minutes*, she thought to herself as she checked the time.

She walked around and climbed back on the hood of the car, sitting cross-legged with her hands on her knees. She closed her eyes and focused on her breathing, quieting her mind, and relaxing her shoulders. She said a prayer of gratitude for the morning.

Some birds in a nearby bush were making a ruckus. She opened her eyes and watched them fly across the pond.

She thought of the women's organization and the next story she had in her mind to write for the ladies. She was enjoying the *She* series she had begun to write, and she loved when she felt inspired to write another addition to it. She said a prayer for the women, hoping they were enjoying them as well.

She leaned back and rested her head on the windshield and started to pray for the day ahead.

"God help me be kind today. Help me to be thoughtful of others and mindful of their feelings," she prayed. She was still nervous she would do something to offend someone at work and find herself without a job once again.

She closed her eyes, letting go of the fear and anxiety this thought brought on. She focused on her breathing, calming her heart and mind as she got ready to focus on the day ahead.

She sat up and looked around one last time, taking in the beauty of the view before her. She felt the slight breeze go through her hair and enjoyed the earthy smells around her for a minute more before she jumped off her car and got in to leave.

As she buckled her seatbelt and started the car, she thought to herself again, *Breathe. Relax. Pray.*

Another day to push forward. There was no time to waste.

~I Had A Complaint~

I had a complaint.

So, I was directed to a guy.

He sort-of stuttered, blushed a bit. He kind of tripped and looked like he had been hit.

And I told him my complaint.

So, I was directed to a guy.

He stared at my boobs. He was awfully crass. He made sexual innuendos. He was a total ass.

And I told him my complaint.

So, I was directed to a guy.

He dyed his hair. He sort-of winked. All the while he talked, I thought ick! What is that stink??

And I told him my complaint.

So, I was directed to a guy.

He flexed his muscles and laughed a lot. All at his own jokes, and he smelled like pot.

And I told him my complaint.

And I was directed to a guy.

He told me of a road to walk. He told me how to watch my talk. His eyes held a spark... and as I felt his passion, they went dark.

His hair fell just so. As I sat for a bit... his voice smooth as honey. It was my turn to feel hit.

The ring on his finger he should have worn proud. His innermost thoughts should never have been said out loud...

And I told him my complaint.

and I was directed to a guy...

Chapter Ten
~David's Corner~

She sat back on David's couch, taking a sip of the vodka/seltzer drink she just made herself.

"You can drink that whole thing if you want." David had said, "Just when that runs out, you will have to settle for Bacardi."

They had both laughed, more so because she probably would end up having Bacardi rather than it being unheard of for her to drink the whole bottle.

Thinking about it now, she smiled.

She and David had a great friendship. He had been her landlord some years back. After the initial year of drunken episodes never leading to sex, they had finally relaxed into a good hang-time balance of sincere friendship.

He was more responsible in a lot of ways that she wasn't. She admired him both as a father and a friend.

They had candid conversations about everything, including sex. She was always interested in listening to his perspective because he was always honest. That didn't mean he was always nice, though he was always himself.

"Hey, I will still bring you to Subway, though I am seriously craving McDonald's, so I still am going to go there." David had come out of the laundry room, folding a towel as he spoke.

She felt her brain freak a bit as she fought with herself to keep her mouth shut and let people live as they felt best. She kept from throwing a million disgusting reasons why this was a very bad idea. Instead, she said, "Ok, that's fine."

"I just want to take a quick shower and then we can go. Just needed to grab a towel. I didn't want to turn you on by walking through the room naked," he laughed as he walked through to the bathroom.

She rolled her eyes and set her head back on the couch. Earlier she had commented how nice his calves were. David was a good-looking guy with a nice physique. He just wasn't her type. His calves were nice though. They reminded her of her friend's calves the one and only time they had hung out casually, playing golf.

David had left the TV on and an episode of Shark Tank was streaming. She focused in on it. She wasn't much of a TV person, though she figured it was the lesser of two evils against her thought process.

The show was talking about a three-sock selling concept. She sat and listened to it for a bit; eyes closed. *TV is so ridiculous,* she said to herself.

She thought through her options for the night. David had offered that she could stay over and sleep on his couch. She did so every now and again. She had to work not far from his house the next morning. It made more sense to stay over here than driving to where she had left her phone the night before. The drive was over an hour and a half away.

"Are you sure you don't mind if I crash here?" she asked as David came out of the bathroom, cleaning his ears with a Q-tip. She smiled to herself, thinking of a silly conversation the two of them had once had about the need for a good Q-tip. "It makes more sense gas-wise, and I will just do some writing."

"Oh, are you going to write about me?" David had asked laughing. "Write that down! Write that down!" Earlier she had commented she was going to start writing a blog called 'David's Advice, From the Real Dad's Perspective.' She really thought he was a great dad. "Of course, I don't mind."

"Oh, by the way, I have a pair of your underwear here."

She quickly wondered which ones and hoped they were decent. She had done her laundry here a few times and had a few boxes of her belongings stored in the back of his laundry room.

"Nice," she said, getting up to head out with him for food.

They went about and got their meals. She was very hungry and ate her food on the way home. She had not been able to just go out and grab what she wanted to eat in a while. Her finances had been non-existent for months. It felt good to be able to have fresh veggies for a change. She said a prayer of gratitude in her head.

David's father was a minister and David had a lot of strong views about religion. She respected that and never tried to make him feel uncomfortable for their differences of opinion. She learned the hard way what it felt like to be alienated for having a different spiritual belief.

She had stopped by David's home spontaneously, having driven to pick up her kids at her ex-husband's house, and finding they both wanted to do something different that night. Having teenagers meant they had their own social schedules. She didn't mind, and she didn't take it personally.

She had not had her phone on her, so she had just popped in without calling first, not something she typically did.

"Hey David, it's me! I just was driving through the area and thought I would see if you felt like hanging for a bit." She had yelled down to him when he called up from his basement.

"Hey, come on down! I am just mudding my basement. It was leaking." He had yelled back up.

She had gone down to his basement and they caught up. She read him a bit about the latest information she had written about the non-profit organization she was working on, along with a few new poems she had written. It was nice to catch up. He shared with her some of the projects he was doing around his house and some work he had lined up.

She sat now, back on the couch, and looked around his home. He always kept it so nice. He wasn't well off by any stretch of the imagination, though he was handy. He had been doing a lot of remodeling to his home.

Her eyes came to rest on a book on his side table. 'Why a Son Needs a Father.' She felt sad inside. David had one of those crazy ex-wives who made selfish decisions based on her own needs. This last year, she and her parents had convinced his teenage son, with money and freedom, to come live with them. David had been a single dad since his son was 6, having had gotten emergency custody when his ex-wife had left her son alone to go out and party. She had had a big drug problem.

"I liked your poem, David." She said to him, very sincerely.

The pain in his face was evident. His son had been his life. He had made some tough decisions after his son continued to disrespect him to let him be. He had been trying to figure out how to deal with this sudden change for over a year now. His son had moved out in the middle of the day while he was at work with no notice to David immediately after he turned 17. David had written a very moving poem for his son a few weeks ago and had sent it to her.

"He is coming up on the 24th." David said, "He said he wants to sit down and talk."

She listened as David filled her in on the latest.

David had been a great help to her this last year. He had gone to a few dealerships and talked on her behalf of her situation and her integrity. She thought of the day she was able to get a ride close to his house and had sat and cried on his couch, frustrated that she had finally found a job and the people who had committed to giving her rides had fallen through. It had been February in New England, and the snowstorms made going out for people by emergency only. Her work situation did not constitute an emergency for anyone but her.

"It sounds like you just need a car, honey." David had said. "Don't you have any connections in the car business?"

She hadn't. The changes in the economy had shifted a lot of the people she had known into different industries. The people she knew still in the business couldn't help with her credit issues. The market was tough for anyone to get a loan, let alone someone who had filed for bankruptcy and just started a new job.

He had wasted no time and quickly found her a car that she could afford at a small mom and pop place.

She would forever be grateful for him. He kept her aware of the reality that even though she was going through a lot, so was most of America. She just needed to deal with it.

She lied back now on the couch, listening to him. Oliver, his dog, walked over and licked her leg.

"Ewww gross, Oliver! NO!" She looked around for a tissue.

"What, did he just lick your leg?" David was laughing. Oliver always did something to gross her out.

"Yes, and his breath stinks." She said, getting up to wash her hands and leg. She had a weak stomach and was trying not to gag.

She came back in as David was tuning in to the TV. *Another reason why we would never have worked as a couple,* she thought to herself as she picked up her notebook. She had dated someone over a year and a half who was a TV guy. She knew it wasn't a lifestyle she wanted.

They sat there in comfortable silence. She wrote in her notebook and ate Doritos. He lied on the other couch smoking cigarettes, watching a Judge Judy episode he had recorded.

She was relaxed and comfortable. It felt nice to stay over there without feeling as though she needed something from him. There was a fine line that came along with male friendships and asking for help, she had found. *Actually, there was a fine line with all friendships and asking for help*, she thought, thinking of the people that were no longer part of her life.

She sat for a minute, thinking of all the help David had given her, and how she enjoyed hearing his viewpoints. She sat for a minute, thinking of the 'lesson' this brought on.

This last year she had learned a lot of 'lessons'. Most of them brought on through humility and surrender. It felt nice to learn a lesson through more of a 'connect the dots' through the last year of pain.

She thought of all she had learned about men's minds when she took the time to explore those instead of what was between their legs.

The key one, she thought to herself, *is that most men are ridiculous.*

And that would be why I am single. She thought as David walked over and put a pillow behind her head so she could crash. *Regardless of how fabulous he may seem.*

DANA VILANDRE

~Sorry... I'm Conboozed~

I laughed for a bit
forgot what she said
went the wrong way
Looking for a different day.
I said goodbye, proceeded to cry
And went to the show anyway.
So, there was booze... and I was confused...
Then my world exploded, and I was conboozed.
Your life isn't so extraordinary.
My life isn't taking your attention away.
And though I have shredded rolls of tissue,
it doesn't change a bit of your day.
My days no longer seem to matter.
My history lived; my promises confirmed.
How extraordinary will my life be defined?
These tissues filled with uncompromised tears.
Tomorrow seems so far away.
When did I accept that I couldn't play this game?
You left me no choice.
Why couldn't it have stayed the same?

This journey of your life is yours to decide.

The way the course will look will be defined from your pride.

Your dreams no longer promise of love and intimacy of your heart.

Locked away, you hold the key. Imprisoned from my own desires,

enslaved I was from the very start.

How to capture it, store it, hold it and call it art.

Expression through words of pad and pen

Chapter Eleven
~The Band~

She sat at the party, listening to the band. The thought crossed her mind that it was a bit bizarre that she and Devon had ended up at a party with a live band, good people and some yummy eats. She had just planned on hanging at the campsite tonight doing some writings for 'Her Story', the 'She' Series for ~HeR PlAcE~.

"Devon, do you want to come for a ride?" It was Mindy. She was pulling a bunch of the kids around the yard in a trailer behind her four-wheeler.

"Sure!" Devon said and jumped up and ran and hopped up onto the trailer.

Amber was sitting next to her. "So hey, do you see your Mr. Right?" she leaned into her and asked.

She laughed. "Where?" she asked. Of course, she was joking. The men here were interested in three things: their wives, their beers, and their trucks. She smiled and leaned back into her chair. She felt so happy to be here. She rested her head back on the chair and took a sip of her wine. She smiled to herself as she recalled her silly hillbilly impersonation she laughed with Amber about earlier because they were drinking wine out of plastic cups.

This year could be described as cheap wine, loud music and lots of ink, she thought to herself.

The night was perfect for an outdoor party. The sky was clear of clouds and the stars were bright without city lights to compete with. The night felt like a fall night in New England, though it was still summer according to the calendar.

The band sounded to her to be a mix of Alice in Chains and the Blues Travelers. Somehow it worked, though she thought that her taste may seem a bit off this last year.

"They must have different neighbors than Kim!" Amber yelled over the music to her. She didn't have much to say about that. That was one of those situations that had been filled with misunderstanding. The type of situation where the worst thing that had happened was how it was handled. She thought through that for a minute, feeling a bit sad. She searched her heart again for what she could have done wrong to hurt her friend's feelings. Again, she felt resolved with her part in it. She said a prayer for her friend and prayed to let it go.

The band started to play a cover of Pearl Jam. She felt the music throughout her spine. She couldn't even begin to explain what these moments felt like.

She had found out yesterday that Amber was coming to this party and that she and Devon were welcome to come along. She knew Mindy, Amber's co-worker who was throwing the party, because Mindy had worked for one of her ex-boyfriends.

"There are going to be people there," Amber had said. "I am just telling you because I know how you feel about being around people. This is definitely a party."

She had felt a wave of guilt at the time. It was true. She didn't want to be around people. She just could not seem to communicate with people anymore. She always seemed to piss them off and wasn't sure why.

"Yea, you are right." She had said. "I am not up for it."

She smiled now, listening to the band and enjoying the company, as she thought of how she and Devon had been lying in a field after leaving the lake by the campground they were staying at. She had sat up just in time to see Amber's car leaving. "Is that Amber?" She had asked Devon. It was. They called out to her and Amber stopped to wait for them.

Amber had dropped off some firewood for her. She had not had her phone on her, so she hadn't received the message Amber was going to stop by.

"So, are you heading over to Mindy's party?" she had asked. She had made a last-minute decision if the invite was still there, she and Devon would go.

"Yea, do you want to come?" Amber had asked.

"Yes, as a matter of fact, we do! Can we just run back to the campsite so I can change first?" She had asked again, pointing to her shorts and tank top which she had worn to the lake.

Now, sitting at the party, she listed as the band moved on to play a song that reminded her of the band Seether. She got up and walked over to peruse the buffet table. Someone had made a home-made potato salad and home-made coleslaw. She made another small plate for herself, feeling incredibly grateful for such delicious food. She walked back to her seat and sat down.

Devon had come back from her ride on the trailer. She watched her daughter for a bit, studying her body language to see if she was coming off snooty. She really respected the way her daughter behaved in public and to new situations. Both of her kids had the ability to adjust quickly to new conditions, and she found them to be kind kids. Her daughter was starting to explore her teen years. She always had to remind herself that her daughter was not reliving her life; her daughter was creating her own life.

She took a deep breath and focused on putting her shoulders back, feeling her chest expand. She took another sip of her wine and continued to enjoy her potato salad and the band.

"Hey there! Do you want to come play volleyball with us?" It was a gentleman she had seen when she had first arrived at the party. They had not been introduced.

"No, thank you," She said and smiled at him. "I am enjoying just sitting here listening to the band. Thank you for asking, though." He stood there for a minute, looking at her oddly. It was almost as though he expected her to say something else.

"Ok. I just heard you were a hot ticket, though I haven't seen that." He trailed off as she continued to smile at him. He turned and went back to the game.

She smiled. She was sore from her new job, and honestly would have loved to play if the night was earlier and the circumstances were different. Tonight, she was only up for relaxing.

She closed her eyes, leaning her head back into her chair and said a prayer of gratitude for her new job. She felt so blessed to have found exactly what she was looking for when she had made the decision to quit her job on the boat and look for work closer to her ex-husband's home. She wanted to be near her kids.

She sat there for a few minutes, listening to the conversations around her and the music; just enjoying the moment. Amber was in a conversation with a cute single guy who had been sitting near them. She smiled as she listened to them talk of his young daughter. She said a prayer of gratitude for being at the party.

God is so good. She thought to herself. *Thank you, God*!

It had been a long year for her and her children. One she never wanted to repeat. She hoped the latest turn of events was in fact the light she glimpsed at the end of the tunnel, and not another mirage filled with false promise as she had felt so many times this year.

She said a prayer, hoping she had turned the page onto a chapter in which she could finally start to breathe again.

Regardless, nothing can predict tomorrow, she thought.

Breathe, Relax, Pray.

~A Date~

I think we should be able to articulate,

when we are out on the loveliest date,

and our defenses are down from being in such a relaxed state,

That maybe the turn-on that you are feeling on this amazing date,

Is the fact he doesn't make you irate.

And perhaps if sex is on his mind and it's getting late,

to be able to say, "Hey, I am sure it would be really great!

Though, really, at this stage. I would rather wait,

to be sure I won't want to choke you in your sleep

after our second date..."

:)

Chapter Twelve
~The Book of James~

She sat in the crowded bar, glass of Pinot Noir in front of her, her notebook open. She was staring at the bottles behind the bar, unseeing, listening to the spattering of conversations going on around her.

There was a couple sitting to her left, not saying much to each other, just short comments about the food and the weather. There was a hurricane that was supposed to hit the area. It was interesting to her that with all the tornados and earthquakes and tsunamis happening lately that people would even comment on a hurricane.

The comments were of concern if they would have enough water and batteries.

There were a couple of women to her right sharing a bottle of wine, the tone of their conversation indicating an intimacy she felt to her core.

She was thinking of the stories she had been writing for the women's group she belonged to. She was thinking it was time to write about James.

She felt her stomach get queasy at the thought of him. *That relationship will be a book in itself*, she thought.

She picked up her glass and sat there for a moment, eyes closed, glass of wine in one hand, pen in the other. She could hear the gentleman on her left sharing about the best way to secure down his belongings. She said a prayer of gratitude to the woman who had opened her home to her just recently. She would hate to think of weathering this storm in her car.

She opened her eyes and took a sip of her wine, tuning back into the conversations around her. The couple to her left had engaged in a conversation with the pretty bartender. The bartender was laughing, telling them a story.

She had been a bartender herself when she was in her early twenties and had enjoyed her interactions with her customers very much. She smiled now, enjoying watching a storyteller in action.

The man the bartender was talking to said something about his home on the island. She tuned in a bit, having had a conversation with a fisherman the day before about the same island. She had wondered what it was like to live on an island.

"Excuse me," she said, smiling at the couple, as well as the bartender, not wanting to seem rude with the interruption. "Did I just hear you say you had a home on the island? I was just talking to someone about that island yesterday. Do you enjoy living there?"

Immediately she realized the place belonged to him, and her interest in the island was more appealing to him apparently than his interest in his date. He went on and on into a story about his custom-built home.

She smiled as she listened, aware of the shift in his date's attitude. She waited out the rest of his talk, smiling.

This is nothing I want to get involved with, she thought to herself.

He finished talking and she made a few meek comments, enough to keep from seeming rude, though definitely not enough to encourage further conversation. The conversation died off, and she looked back down at her notebook.

She was startled by a hand on her waist. She looked up as the sexy bartender leaned into her so she could be heard to ask if she wanted some rolls to eat.

She felt a flash of energy run through her body. She quickly reminded herself that just because she felt someone's energy it did not mean it was sexual.

She relaxed into her answer. "Yes, thank you."

She went back to her notebook, smiling, thinking of a conversation she had with her friend suggesting she should date women. She laughed to herself thinking of the lesser of the two evils. Men, she could understand. She knew that she herself was unpredictable, and she certainly didn't want to deal with another woman's hormones.

She smiled now, thinking of all the sexy, sassy women and the discussion group they had formed. She always enjoyed their intelligence and feedback. She found them to be fun.

She refocused on the story she wanted to write for them. *Where do I start with a story like this?* she thought.

James had been a very bad choice of a man for her and her children to be involved with. He had come into her life at a time she was struggling; financially, but more importantly, spiritually. She had been very sincere in her walk with her Creator. Due to making some hard choices and changes in her life that went against the church's common belief, she had chosen to walk away from what she felt was expected of her to maintain a relationship with God.

She sat back now and took a long sip of wine. She thought of the things she had shared with the women in the group. She was incredibly open with them about her life. She knew she would always want to be. She was always looking for the balance of boundaries, while respecting other's lives are theirs to live.

She thought again about James. When she met him, she had been fed up with the dating scene, having had been on one of those dating websites and not enjoying the men she felt like she could hand-pick from it. It had seemed as though they all had issues, though most certainly they thought she was the one who had issues. She had been hurt a few times romantically. Looking back over their relationship, James represented a complete breakdown of her own moral behavior.

The ladies next to her paid their bill and left. Another gentleman came in and sat down a seat over from her. She looked over to see him checking her out, looking her up and down. She smiled, more just a lift of her mouth, and looked back down at her notebook. She had just been through a rapid-fire series of men come into her life. She had no desire to explore another package.

I am definitely on a sabbatical, she thought to herself. She refocused on her time spent with James, the boyfriend from Hell.

She hated to think she had been in a relationship with him. She hated even more how long she stayed in that relationship. She knew he was not a nice man. She hated how she felt about herself for introducing him to her children.

~Butterfly~

What is this? You and I?
I didn't recognize you as a butterfly!
I didn't know that you watched,
Or had a seat by my side.
While the tears had been spent, and the sorrows were dried.
What is this? You and I?
Why the heart so drawn and raw?
Even words of basic understanding
Read like poetry and look like fine art
So poetic are the sounds
Though the words are rarely profound.
It must be a dream I was trapped within!
Time shows it will happen, again and again.
What is this? You and I?
Today I am free
No person I am bound to
Yet my heart has been sliced a million times
With memories never lived through.

Chapter Thirteen
~Roula's Restaurant~

She finished reading the story and looked up at Louie. His eyes looked watery, though that was normal for him.

"Is that all you got?" He asked her in his grumpy eighty-four-year-old way.

Louie was one of those little old men who no one paid much attention to, so he often found his attention from others by being rude to them. She had liked him immediately.

"What do you mean 'is that all I have'?" She had asked him, teasing. She had already given him quite a few of her stories. It made her happy that he enjoyed reading them. She knew he was alone, and she knew he was lonely.

"Ok, handsome, I need to get back to work. Would you like anything else?"

"Who are you?" He asked, "You are not my waitress!" He said, smiling. This was a going joke between them.

"Ok, sir," She stood up and bowed slightly, smiling. "I will see if we can find her for you."

They had both laughed as she walked back to the counter to check on the other patrons.

"Excuse me, are you a writer?" A gentleman who had been sitting with his back to them a few booths over asked her.

"Yes," She spoke more over her shoulder as she walked back to the counter to get a cloth to wipe down a table. "I guess you could say that." She smiled over at him as she picked up the cloth and got a new table setting ready.

"What is it you write?" He asked.

The table she had needed to clear was near him, so she was able to continue to talk without feeling rude.

"Oh, I write a bit of everything." She answered. "Philosophy, political, poems, short stories. Whatever pops into my head."

"Oh! Are you published?" He had stopped eating and was really focusing on her. She wondered briefly if he was going to try and pick her up. This happened a lot with men and she often found herself having to word things wisely, so she wasn't misleading them. She was a friendly woman who enjoyed people, and she often found men misinterpreted kindness and sincerity as a more personal interest. She didn't feel this vibe from him, though. He seemed sincerely curious.

"No, actually. I enjoy writing, though writing is not my primary focus," she had answered. "I have been creating a women's non-profit for the last year and a half. That is my real goal."

She finished clearing and setting the table then went back to put the cloth in the water bucket. She took a walk around the restaurant to check on the other patrons. A new couple came in and sat down, and she went about waiting on them. After they were settled and their food order was taken, she had walked again around the restaurant to be sure everyone was all set.

She was back in front of the gentleman who had asked about her writings.

"This non-profit", He picked the conversation back up. "What is it about?"

She had laughed a little. There wasn't really a clearly defined answer to this yet.

"Hmm, well now, that's a good question." She said, laughing a bit. "It has grown quite a bit and evolved from what I first imagined it would be. I guess you could say it is an organization of women who deal with life issues in real ways, while supporting other women to do the same without judgment or a fixer attitude. It is called 'Her Place.' It's a bit more involved than that though."

"That is so interesting!" He had said. "I work for the local TV station. Would you be interested in perhaps being on one of our shows as a guest, and then maybe having your own program?"

"Wow, that sounds like fun!" She had said. "Seriously?"

"Yes," he had said. "As a matter of fact, on Thursday, we will meet with another non-profit, if you would like to come down to the station and see what it is all about."

"Oh, wow. That sounds great!"

"Excuse me, miss, can I have some more coffee?" A customer at a table nearby asked, holding up his coffee cup.

"Sure!" She answered, smiling. "Excuse me again." She said to the gentleman. "What is your name, by the way?" She held her hand out.

"Pete," he answered, shaking her hand.

"Nice to meet you!"

She turned and went to get the coffee pot. She filled the gentleman's cup and went around the restaurant to see if anyone else needed refills or anything else from her.

A few more patrons started to come in and she got busy for a while. It happened like that, being a waitress. Quiet one minute. Then running around, busy the next. She had gotten caught up in the moment and had forgotten about Pete and the TV station until he was standing at the register to pay his bill.

"So, how was everything?" She asked, smiling, taking his slip to ring up.

"Great," he said, though he seemed distracted. "Would you like to do that this Thursday? Come down to the station, that is."

"Yes, I think that should work," She answered. "I would like to bring a couple of the other women with me, if that is okay. Does any particular time work best?"

"They are meeting with the other non-profits in the afternoon, though you can come by and have a tour of the studio, and we can talk more, given the morning time works best for you."

"Well, I cannot really focus right now because I am at work. Can I have your number and call you on Thursday with the time? Or should we plan it out for next week?"

"We are pretty flexible, so this week will work," he answered. "I think you would be great to have your own program. You are quite interesting. Most people are boring."

She smiled at him. "Thank you," she put her hand out again. "It was very nice to meet you! I look forward to talking more."

He took her hand and shook it, smiling. "You as well," he said, "I think this will be a very good thing." And with that, he turned and walked out the door.

~The Dino~

~As I sat by a stream, passing the time, a two-legged dinosaur walked up, sat down and started to rhyme.

He said, "Hey there, do you remember me? I was teaching you to ROAR when you were just three! I loved to see you all silly and fun, playing and loving up on everyone!" With that, he stood and danced about, did a jitterbug, shuffled his tail to and fro, sat back down and looked deep in thought.

He went on, his voice sounding grave, his next words making me seem brave, "It didn't matter how things seemed to be so hard in your life. You played and loved and looked to dissolve strife. I watched you make new friends, let some old ones go. You learned lots of fun lessons learning to go with your flow."

He then sat back, put his large head on his fist, his arm on his dino knee, his eyes starting to mist. "I watched you cry when grownups said 'enough is enough! Life isn't about playing! You better get tough!'"

Finally, he stopped and looked over at me, as though surprised. My mouth was wide open, I could hardly speak, and he must have seen the shock in my eyes!

I regained my composure. Surely this couldn't be! This talking dinosaur, sitting, talking, and dancing for me?

Though as my heart slowed down and I relaxed in the sun, this dino looking at me like he was the innocent one, I did recall a day in my past that I did feel so free! That I truly liked to roar, and call myself three!

I sat there, remembering a minute more, recalling for a minute what it felt like to roar.

I closed my eyes, remembering the days when I was first discovering me, enjoying the thought that a dino that rhymes could be sitting next to me. I thought how silly it would be to say, that in my adventures out and about, a dino had come my way? Dinos don't actually sit by streams! Well, I have only seen them in my dreams.

Though I sat there that warm summer day, and I wondered what if a walking dino could talk to me, what would he say? I would think that my three-year-old self is really missed, and I think the things that have come about in life, may have made that three-year-old feel dissed. The grownups I met, the ones in my day to day, all had great hearts, they all had great things to say! Though they weren't searching, they weren't living, they weren't loving as me, so they didn't really understand who I was looking to be.

SO, I was happy to have this make-believe friend, who came by the stream, and was an ear I could bend. This laughing, talking, dancing dino that I made up in my mind, helping me to remember, not to leave that fun loving three-year-old, so far behind"~

Chapter Fourteen
~Dancing with Mary~

"We can always go to the store and pick something up to cook back at my brother's place," TD was looking at her as he said it. She was thinking perhaps he wasn't sure how she would react.

This was the first time they were meeting face-to-face after a year of corresponding by mail. It would be normal for him to wonder if this was too forward a thing to suggest on a first meeting.

"That works!" She answered, though she did feel a bit disappointed they would not be eating out. She had a craving for steak tip subs and had found a place close by where they weren't very expensive buy them from. TD knew her finances were tight, and she knew he really was not financially able to afford to be eating out either.

She had become pen-pals with TD after meeting through an ex-boyfriend on Facebook. TD was a musician and had shown interest in some charitable work she had been investing her time in when they both had hit some personal roadblocks in their lives that had left them distanced from people. They had been sharing at a pretty personal level through mail while they both struggled to find their footing again in life. Even though this was their first meeting face to face, they both felt more connected to each other because they had shared so openly and honestly all year.

They went to the grocery store and picked up some groceries. The cost was more than she anticipated.

"Well, if you don't mind, my brothers and Mary will all be at the house when we get there. We can make a big dish for everyone," TD suggested. "It would still work out to be the same price as if we had chosen to eat out, but now we are going to be able to feed three more." She hadn't thought about his family being there when they reached his home. It made a lot more sense to buy food to cook for everyone.

They finished up at the store and headed back to his brother's townhouses. As they drove, he talked a bit about his brothers and how much they had been there for him over the last year. He brought up his brother Don's name. She instantly felt annoyed.

"You know, I have to say, he was kind of a dink to me," she said, cutting him off, not thinking about it. "He came across really disrespectful of you once on a Facebook posting I had."

"Don can just come off that way," TD said, looking out his passenger window.

He didn't say anything for a minute, and she started to feel a bit bad for bashing his brother. She didn't know his brother, or any of their history. Who was she to make a judgment call about how his brother responded to a Facebook posting?

"He really went through hell to get Mary back," TD went on after a couple of seconds. "He got himself into a lot of trouble a few years back and got arrested. The day after he was incarcerated, his ex-wife brought Mary down to Social Services and said she couldn't handle her anymore and left her there. When he got out of jail it took him two years to get custody of her back."

He stopped talking again. Now she really felt bad. TD was a very spiritual guy, and throughout the year, his songs and letters had kept her company when she didn't have anyone else to talk to. She thought again to herself how easy it is to be caught up in her own issues and not stop and think of what other people are going through.

Her heart felt sad as she sat there and thought about Mary. How sad and confusing for the little girl to try and understand why her parents had been in her life one minute, then gone the next.

They pulled into the townhouse and walked in right behind Mary getting home from school. Mary was standing in the small dining room taking off her coat. She immediately put her hand out to Mary and walked over.

"Hello, Mary," She said, taking Mary's little hand in her own and shaking it, very grown up and on purpose. "I am a friend of your Uncle Tyler."

Mary shook her hand and giggled, ducking her head into her shoulder a bit. TD, or Uncle Tyler as Mary knew him, walked by them carrying the groceries into the kitchen.

"Mary, she is going to stay and have dinner with us tonight!" He called over his shoulder as he went through.

Mary dropped her hand and went quickly to the dining room table, climbing up on one of the chairs to reach into the book bag she had dropped there as she had come in.

"Look what I got in school today!" Mary pulled out a sheet of paper filled with green stars.

"Mary gets those when she completes all of her assignments for the week." Someone said from behind her. She jumped a bit. She hadn't heard someone come in. She turned and put out her hand to the gentleman now in front of her.

"Hello! You must be one of Tyler's brothers?" she asked, taking his hand and shaking it, smiling as she did.

"Yes, I am Paul," he said, smiling back. "We talked on Facebook before."

"Oh, yes, you are right."

She turned her attention back to Mary. "That is awesome, Mary! Do you like school?" She was curious about her. She had met quite a few children in the last year that had gone through a lot of challenges with their home lives. Mary's situation seemed so sad to her. She imagined she must really miss having a mom around, or even a woman. She was only seven years old. She felt so sad to think she didn't have any women in her life.

Mary smiled and tucked her head again into her shoulder. Mary seemed to be sizing her up.

"Daddy!" Mary's face lit up as the door opened again behind her. TD's other brother Don walked in.

She felt the instant stab of annoyance as she recalled the interaction they had had last year. She said a quick prayer to let it go and smiled as she walked towards him, her hand once again extended.

"Hello! You must be Don!" she said, as they approached each other. He was a bit odd, and she realized quickly he was slow. She felt a small wave of irritation with herself for being so annoyed with a little interaction over a Facebook posting. She felt a bit ridiculous for it.

They all talked for a few minutes, Mary hanging on Don as they did, as any typical seven-year-old would do who was happy to have their dad's attention for a few minutes.

After a short bit of time, TD announced that dinner was ready. They all went into the kitchen, made a plate then went back to the table to eat.

Mary was a picky eater and finished her specialty plate of chicken nuggets and tator-tots before the rest of them had finished with their meals. She sat at the table, fidgety, waiting for everyone to finish.

"So, Mary, do you like to draw?" She was interested to know if Mary had any creative outlets. It seemed to her some of the most creative people she knew were able to take their circumstances that were less than ideal and turn them into some form of art. She had found it quite an incredible experience to tap into these kids' minds over last year. Despite their challenging upbringings they had expressed themselves through art.

Mary again acted shyly and nodded her head a bit.

She pulled a notebook out of her book bag and picked up a pencil that had been sitting on the dinner table near them. She gave them both to Mary. Mary drew while they finished eating.

After dinner, she was in the kitchen helping clean the dinner plates. She was talking quietly with TD as they washed and put away the dishes.

"Can I show you something?" It was Mary. She had changed into a dress and had a CD in her hand.

"Oh, Mary! Are we going to dance?" she asked the little girl. She was so happy! She loved to dance, and it warmed her heart that Mary had come back out to get her. Mary smiled and nodded, taking her hand and pulling her through the hall into her bedroom.

Mary's room was a bit barren for a little girl's room and not picked up. She felt a flash of sadness, again, that Mary didn't have anyone in the house who would understand how important it is to have a pretty room. She made a mental note to come back someday and help Mary decorate. As she thought of this, she smiled, thinking her teenage daughter would love to do just that with her.

Mary stood by the door for a minute. She looked over at her.

"Is it okay if I shut the door?" Mary asked.

A thought went through her mind that no one here really knew her. She wondered how they would feel about Mary shutting the door. She thought through this for a minute, knowing Mary was too shy to dance in front of them, and wanted the door shut so that they wouldn't see her.

She made her decision based on faith.

"Is it because you are shy to dance with it open?" She asked her, hoping she had said it loud enough for TD to hear. Mary nodded her head and shut the door. She went over to the CD player and put in the CD she had been holding. After a second, a song started she was not familiar with.

Mary stood shy, fidgeting a bit with her fingers in her mouth.

"Well now, standing there with your fingers in your mouth isn't dancing!" She said, smiling, and she herself started to dance around the room, all silly, laughing and taking Mary's little hands for her to dance with her. Mary laughed as they danced around the room for the whole song. She spun Mary around, teaching her some waltz and cha-cha moves as the music played on. It felt as if the room was glowing as they danced and laughed, spinning and being silly, just enjoying the fun in it all. The music came to an end and she gave Mary a couple of final spins, while Mary laughed and spun away.

"Who are you?" Mary asked, laughing as she looked back over at her. Mary's face was lit up and happy. She felt as though her heart had been bear-hugged with the amount of joy Mary's smile instilled in her.

"Why, I am Dana, honey! You know that!" She laughed as she answered her. She walked over to re-open the door, feeling her shoulders relax as she did. She didn't know them well, and though she was pretty sure they would see her time with Mary for what it was, she didn't want to take the chance of someone misinterpreting her kindness.

She turned back to Mary, giving her a deep curtsy as she did.

"Thank you, M'lady, for the lovely dance!" she said, using a fake British accent.

And she turned and walked out of the room, listening to Mary's giggles as she left.

~How to make a snowman~

To make a snowman, first there needs to be just the right snow. Use the type of snow that clumps together, so with a press it forms into something more. To make a snowman, the day must be snowy weather.

Next step in making a snowman, after assuring the flakes clump together, would be to think of what you want your snowman to look like. Do you want your snowman large? Small? Fat? Tall? I would think to make a snowman you would really want to know this all.

After the picture in your mind is loud and clear, the following step will make you a little more aware. Take the snow in your hands and clump it just so. Then once it sticks solid, start rolling along the snow so it will grow.

Keep rolling until you find the right size, creating the first layer of the snowman that you visualized.

The next layer is easier still. Again, you will start to roll the ball of clumped up snow, again watching it grow.

Layer two is now done. You put them together. Now it is a two-ball stack that is only going to get better.

So again, take your hands, fill them with the white, cold, wintery stuff, and keep rolling that clumped-up piece until it is enough.

The third is the smallest, and light as a feather, so you want to put it on top, as you put them all together.

Now stand back and admire your work, for surely you are not done, so do not go berserk.

It needs a face, some character to it, now let's start with a carrot and some buttons, yes, it is all starting to fit.

A scarf still it needs, maybe a hat already worn. The snowman before for its dress will never be shorn.

A nose, perhaps a carrot? Maybe a pipe it needs as well. Hmm... now let's step back and take a look. Yes, this snowman indeed should be in a book! Though no accolades or agreements I need you to say, because as far as building a snowman, well this was the easiest way.

Chapter Fifteen
~No Price Tags, No Paychecks~

She sat, staring at the keys, in thought.

Too much thinking, she thought.

She closed her eyes, concentrating on relaxing her brain. She started to breathe slowly and deliberately, in through the nose, out through the mouth.

She opened her eyes, stood up and set her laptop down. She walked over to the patio door that overlooked the lake.

She sat in front of it, cross-legged and staring out over the picture-perfect scene the lake and tree line made before her.

What a year! She thought to herself.

It had been a year ago that she had moved back in with family and started to rebuild her own life. It had been just over six months since she had been in a place of her own once again.

She glanced over at the stack of notebooks that sat not far from her side. She looked back over the lake and closed her eyes to stop the feeling of anxiety that started to rise in up in her chest. Her passion for continuing to create the organization at times felt like her very nemesis.

She thought of last two years. Her heart long ago resolved with her choices, yet the layer of sadness was still there.

She stood up again and looked around the room. Her home.

Her phone went off, there was a message from a friend on Facebook. She smiled to herself and thought of her comment in a group the night before where she said she needed to divorce Facebook.

She walked about her home, looking at the few items she had hung about. An astrology calendar, a poster which to her symbolized soul-searching, and the first poster she displayed at a public outreach event for the non-profit.

Her mind returned to the business plan she was working on, and the next steps to move the organization forward.

A place to just be me.

She walked back into her room, sat down on a chair that faced the poster she and her daughter had created. She picked back up her laptop and turned it on.

As she waited for it to boot, her thoughts returned to the events that had happened over the last year. She thought about all the business meetings she pulled together and the documents she had composed. She thought of the work she had invested in the non-profit to date.

She thought of all she had still to do.

It was time.

Just to be me, she thought again of these words.

The laptop came to life, and she clicked open the file with the manuscript she had been working on for so long. Her journey. She hadn't read through it since her last edit six months before, embarrassed by the recorded words documenting the pain her own heart had held on to.

Healing.

The word rang in her mind, the realization that the very home she looked to create for women was, in fact, her own solace. A place which she had created to find the time to heal.

She stopped for a moment and stood up, setting the laptop down again. She walked back over to look out over the lake.

The view before her was beautiful and so peaceful. She thought to herself how fortunate she was. She closed her eyes and prayed that she could create a place for all women who needed it to find such a space. A place to sort through their pain, and to pick up the pieces and put their lives back together.

She knew, to move to the next step, she had to finish the last steps. She needed to finish documenting for others to experience her work. She stood there for a minute more, feeling her own frustrations toward the mistakes she had made, well aware of the mental battles she went through to move past them all.

She went back to her chair, picked up the laptop and again began to type. As she typed the final words that would close out her chapter of a lost love she will have to do without, she knew the creation of the organization was now ready to convey the love she found within.

GYPSY NOMAD HIPPIE CHICK

www.ingramcontent.com/pod-product-compliance
Lightning Source LLC
Chambersburg PA
CBHW031115080526
44587CB00011B/982